THE MAGIC
OF THINKING BIG
IN SELLING

BY

JON DOHERTY

WITH

ROBERT G. HOEHN

PRENTICE-HALL, INC.
ENGLEWOOD CLIFFS, NJ

Prentice-Hall International, Inc., *London*
Prentice-Hall of Australia, Pty. Ltd., *Sydney*
Prentice-Hall Canada, Inc., *Toronto*
Prentice-Hall of India Private Ltd., *New Delhi*
Prentice-Hall of Japan, Inc., *Tokyo*
Prentice-Hall of Southeast Asia Pte. Ltd., *Singapore*
Whitehall Books, Ltd., *Wellington, New Zealand*
Editora Prentice-Hall do Brasil, Ltda., *Rio de Janeiro*

Library of Congress Cataloging in Publication Data

Doherty, Jon
The magic of thinking big in selling.

1. Selling. I. Hoehn, Robert G. II. Title.
HF5438.25.D63   1983   658.8′5   83-4526

ISBN 0-13-545285-6
ISBN 0-13-545210-4 {PBK}

HOW THIS BOOK WILL HELP YOU CASH IN AS A "BIG THINKER" SALESPERSON

You Are What You Think—So Think Big, Sell Big

All topflight salespeople have one thing in common: a burning desire to sharpen their selling skills and earn really big money in the selling game.

The Magic of Thinking Big in Selling shows you—the experienced salesperson—fresh, field-tested methods that virtually guarantee a sale every time! This practical guide works hand in hand with you. It:

- Shows how to create a selling character that will prepare you, mentally and physically, for the acting role of a super salesperson.
- Gives you a step-by-step approach on how to establish and reach personal goals that will bring you superior results (Chapter 1).
- Presents a unit (Chapter 1) on how to catapult your earnings by employing a big thinker's formula for success.
- Offers stimulating ideas, suggestions, and secrets for upgrading your sales presentation. Chapter 2, "The Magic of Setting the Stage for Big Sales," presents unique ways for handling prospects and shows how to effectively demonstrate products.
- Pinpoints practical ways to deal with the mental and physical aspects of cold calling. You'll discover how big-thinking salespeople turn cold calling into money-making projects (Chapter 3).

- Discloses super selling techniques that will put you on top to stay. Chapter 4, "Building and Maintaining a Big Thinker's Selling Package," stresses outstanding ways to clinch big sales and offers solid, down-to-earth ideas that you can start using today! This chapter is an accumulation of 20 years of sales experience.

- Shows how a clever salesperson can combine tact and timing to change a "No" response into a definite "Yes" (Chapter 5). As a special bonus, this unit—"A Big Thinker's Approach to Handling Objections"—offers a foolproof plan to keep you selling over and over again.

- Reveals sure-fire closing techniques. Chapter 6, "Developing Ironclad Strategies for Closing Sales," gives you proven successful methods for closing big sales and tells you when to use them in what selling situation. You'll receive solid advice on ways to avoid the stumbling blocks famous for killing sales.

- Triggers the power of humor in successful selling. Chapter 7, "Selling Big With the Magic of Humor," arms you with profitable tips and suggestions on how timely humor can help you close that big sale.

- Offers practical tips on how to smell out and handle those tricky problems that appear from time to time. You'll see how to handle the selling slump and regain full control of your selling character. And best of all, you'll learn effective ways to keep your selling character in tiptop shape (Chapter 8).

- Demonstrates effective communication techniques. In Chapter 9, "Big Thinking Selling Strategies for Keeping Yourself on Target," you'll learn how to increase your earnings by improving your communication skills.

- Identifies the problem of "selling burnout." Chapter 10, "Recognizing and Preventing Selling Burnout," explains the symptoms of burnout and tells you how to treat it if it happens to you.

Throughout the book, we present case studies, charts, illustrations, and checklists, which have been carefully selected to help you mold a bright future as a big-thinking super salesperson.

Jon Doherty
with Robert G. Hoehn

CONTENTS

CHAPTER ONE

THINKING BIG PAYS OFF IN THE SELLING GAME

A mountain climber, like a big-thinking salesperson, prepares mentally and physically to face the challenge of reaching the top. However, once a mountain climber reaches the summit, he turns his attention to heading down the mountain. Conversely, a big-thinking salesperson searches for ways to stay on top, to reign as King of the Mountain.

Big thinking. That's the key to successful sales. You'll run across this phrase often as you study and practice the selling techniques revealed in the chapters that follow.

The Magic of Thinking Big in Selling shows you, the wise salesperson, how to clinch major sales, and perhaps best of all, how to consistently send your profit margin spiraling upward. You'll receive sound tips and money-making suggestions for sharpening your selling technique.

Selling, as you know, requires long hours of hard practice. You must be willing to put these ideas into action and let them work for you. Andrew Carnegie said, "There is no use whatever trying to help people who do not help themselves. You cannot push anyone up a ladder unless he is willing to climb himself."

The Magic of Thinking Big in Selling provides the building blocks, the rungs up the ladder of successful salesmanship. Study them. Practice them. Take them one step at a time.

A BIG THINKER'S SUCCESS FORMULA

Big-thinking salespeople make big money in the selling game. That's a simple, direct statement. Yet only a small percentage of salespeople fall into the high-income bracket. Why?

Salespeople begin their careers boiling over with enthusiasm, extruding enough energy to light up New York City for years to come. Then, for some, the luster tarnishes, the light fades, and optimism dwindles. Why?

Simply, these salespeople fail to apply a big thinker's success formula, which is: Set realistic goals for yourself. Then program your thinking to reach each goal in a minimal amount of time with maximal effort.

Three years ago a friend of mine rushed into my office with a foolproof get-rich plan. I had never seen him so excited. He had tried selling everything from used cars to encyclopedias. He made approximately $15,000 a year.

The plan, like so many others, promised to earn him $50,000 or more a year *if* he conscientiously applied the suggested techniques. The program required an initial investment *plus* a substantial amount of time to energize the plan.

My friend grabbed the bait and headed for open water. Unfortunately the plan fizzled, he lost his investment, and now he's back at the starting line.

What happened? Couldn't the plan have succeeded? In a word, yes. But my friend made the same mistake hundreds of others make: He thought he could get rich by expending a minimum amount of energy and hard work.

Well, maybe you're not naive enough to delude yourself into thinking big money comes easily, but that's exactly why so many people leave the selling profession each year—they don't earn enough big money to keep their dreams alive.

How can you, an experienced salesperson, double or triple your yearly income? How can the big-thinker's formula pay off for you? The next five sections will prepare you to meet the challenge of becoming a highly successful, big-thinking salesperson.

TAKING A GOOD, HARD LOOK AT YOURSELF

The first step in preparing yourself for big-thinking action is to take a good, hard look at yourself. Here's how:

1. Step in front of a mirror. Ask yourself these questions:
- Am I really happy in my present job?
- Am I attaining what I set out to accomplish?
- Am I selling enough to earn big money year after year?

- Am I providing adequately for my family?

If you answer no to any of these items, then ask yourself: Why not? Is it my product? Is it my company? Or could it be ... me?

2. Reexamine your motives for entering the selling field. Maybe you're happy making $15,000 or $20,000 a year. Perhaps you don't have the determination or discipline to shoot for higher stakes. That's fine, just don't mesmerize yourself into thinking somebody else is keeping you from earning big money. Conversely, if you're unhappy with your performance, now's the time to do something about it.

CHANGING THE WAY YOU THINK

The second step involves reestablishing your thinking pattern. From this point on you must mold every thought around two giant words: THINK BIG. Here's how to begin:

A. Make a case study of a salesperson you know fairly well who consistently leads others in sales and collects sizable bonus checks at regular intervals.

Start by getting a pencil and a 3 by 5 index card. Put your subject's name at the top of the card and make a list of personality traits that you feel help your subject score big sales, for example, assertive, sense of humor, confident, innovative, and so on.

Now number one through ten on the card. Read each of the following questions and write "yes" or "no" after each number on the card.

1. Does subject feel that making sales and being productive supersede having friends and doing things with others?

2. Does a high income and being a top salesperson influence subject's work?

3. Does subject overshadow others in confidence, optimism, and endurance?

4. Does subject shake off failures easily?

5. Does subject persuade and influence others at sales meetings and social gatherings?

6. Does subject attain positive selling results without using force?

7. Does subject constantly seek ways to improve selling technique?

8. Does subject plan ahead and set goals within the scope of reality?

9. Does subject follow a definite plan of attack with enough flexibility to adjust when necessary?

10. Does subject prepare mentally and physically for meeting prospects?

Your subject will likely fall into the "yes" category for all items. Therefore it's safe to say that your subject is definitely a big-thinking high achiever who possesses such powerful personality traits as self-confidence, assertiveness, and durability.

B. Underline two or three of your subject's personality traits that *you* desire to develop within yourself.

C. Focus attention on your first choice. Collect, read, and study magazine articles or books covering your top selection.

D. Include the suggestions gleaned from your readings into your sales presentation. Go slowly at first. Give them a chance to work. After a reasonable amount of time, weed out the sludge and concentrate on those items that bring positive results. An important point to remember is: Focus your efforts into one good area intensively until it starts paying off.

E. Surround yourself with people who share your enthusiasm and ambition. This keeps the big-thinking success machine running smoothly.

F. Keep in mind that you are what you think, and since thought precedes action, here's a simple, one-line message for you to repeat over and over to yourself:

I'm a confident, big-thinking salesperson.

Say it. Believe it. Then practice it. If you continually feed your brain positive stimuli, you will respond in a positive manner.

To stress a point, several years ago I worked as a sales manager for a roofing and insulation firm in Los Angeles. The salesperson I assigned to cover the north section of the territory failed to write a single contract in five days. He claimed "slum dwellers" in a depressed area aren't receptive prospects, therefore it's useless to try to sell anything.

I decided to give the area a try. Within one week seven families had signed a contract to have the company service their needs.

The sales person failed because he thoroughly convinced himself that nobody would buy; consequently he didn't really try. The area came alive for me because I knew people needed our services. Hence, I approached each prospect with a positive selling attitude. In short, *thinking big pays off big* in the selling game.

G. Repeat Steps C through F for your second and third choices. In time you'll pull together a big-thinking power package bulging with unlimited money-making potential.

RESELLING YOURSELF

You must keep your big-thinking selling machine ready for action at all times. Your goal, as a big-thinking salesperson, is to double or triple your earning power. In order for this to happen, you must resell yourself on the idea that a great selling future lies ahead. This requires a conscientious effort on your part to break from the comfortable groove, which offers security, but severely limits your high-earning potential. So here's your challenge: Gird yourself to push hard, drive forward, and earn a big-thinker's reputation. You can resell yourself in the following manner:

1. Reexamine your present goals

What did you hope to gain by entering the selling profession? Think hard. Now test your memory by listing those rewards on a piece of paper. For example, your list might look like this:

- To earn $60,000 a year
- To own a late-model sports car
- To become business manager

Let's suppose you had given yourself three years to reach these goals, but, unfortunately, you didn't make it. In fact, you earn $18,000 a year, drive a Chevrolet (four years old), and your company recently hired a person from out of state to manage your department.

Your goals missed the runway because they sprang from a

wish, not reality. It's almost like trying to build a house without plans. Big thinking requires intelligent planning, common sense, and working smart.

So make sure your goals are realistic and attainable within a reasonable amount of time. This will keep you from losing interest and allowing apathy to gain a foothold.

2. Make a total commitment to reach your objectives

Arm yourself with strong, positive statements like I *can*, I *will*, and I *must*.

3. Build enthusiasm within your mental machinery

How? By really liking what you are doing. Enthusiasm breeds positive energy, which, in turn, sets loose the driving force necessary to catapult you into higher earnings.

Three ways of building enthusiasm are:

- Picture yourself as a hard-working, goal-oriented person heading for the top.
- Develop a work schedule around an atmosphere of cheerful people who express a willingness to help one another.
- Think happy thoughts.

4. Apply the four Ds of selling success

The Four *Ds* of selling success—desire, determination, dedication, and discipline—are major factors in developing and maintaining a big-thinker's attitude. Use them wisely. Let them help you build a powerful selling package.

KEEPING YOURSELF ON TRACK

Once you get your big-thinking machine in motion, you must steer a straight course for immediate action. In other words, you must sidestep those obstacles that are famous for snuffing out enthusiasm and turning dreams into nightmares. How can you keep yourself on track and headed in the right direction? Following are four ways.

1. Set a tangible plan of attack

If you expect to double or triple your income in two years, establish a realistic plan laced with opportunities for you to reach your objective. These opportunities, for example, might include attending workshops, seminars, and training sessions; going to school or taking correspondence courses; interviewing highly successful salespeople; working with community leaders; playing an active role in service organizations; and staying abreast of modern selling techniques by reading timely magazine articles, newsletters, and books. None of these things, however, will be much help unless you ferret out the nuggets and plug them into your game plan.

2. Stick to your game plan

Remember your new, big-thinking objective, which is to double or triple your income. You've activated your success mechanism by creating a tangible plan for reaching your objective. So give your plan sufficient time to work. Patience and persistence lead to productivity. If you allow certain negative forces like doubt and self-pity to creep into your game plan, you'll become confused, lose control, and wind up back at the starting line.

3. Put your plan in writing

A big-thinking Master Plan comes to life the moment it hits the drawing board. By writing down everything you intend to accomplish you give direction and purpose to your career.

As an example, during my first year of selling I worked for a red hot, "go get 'em" sales manager who ate sugar-coated positrons for breakfast. His philosophical tidbits spewed forth in pluses. He'd say things like, "Okay, people, tell yourself that Mr. Negative no longer exists. Once you kick him out of your thoughts, you'll open new cranial spaces for positive thinking." Then he'd cap off his statement with, "...and you'll stay positive if you write down, read over, and study your intentions."

An excellent point. In fact, here's one of his suggestions that *really* works:

Take a 3 by 5 index card and write the following message in black ink:

When there is nothing to lose and everything to gain—sell, sell, sell. Do it now!

At the bottom of the same card print these words again in red ink:

<u>Do</u> it <u>now</u>! Underline each word.

Scotch tape the card in plain view of the dashboard of your automobile. Repeat these words often as you drive about. Form a mental picture of the message in your mind's eye. Condition your mind to accept only one thing: making the sale.

By writing down your intentions you're saying to yourself, "I'm serious about reaching my big-thinking objective." Your Master Plan might look something like this:

MASTER PLAN

A. Big-thinking objective—major goal
    To earn $68,000 in the next two years.
B. Goal statements—what I intend to accomplish while working toward big-thinking objective.
    1. Update and improve selling skills
    2. Increase concentration and money-making aspect of selling
    3. Keep a big-thinking, positive outlook on selling
    4. Keep track of earnings on a daily, weekly, and monthly basis
C. How will I reach my goal statements?
    1. I will update and improve my selling skills by attending workshops and seminars on proven selling techniques.
    2. I will increase my concentration on the money-making aspect of selling by taking a correspondence course entitled *Boost Your Earnings Through Selling Dynamics* and by reading and studying several magazine articles and books designed to boost self-confidence and positive thinking.
    3. I will keep a big-thinking, positive outlook on selling by writing down my intentions so they will serve as a constant reminder to push forward, drive hard, and never give up. I'll keep these reminders posted in conspicuous places— dashboard of my car, office wall, above the doorway at home, and so on.

4. I will keep track of earnings by listing the amount of money earned at different time intervals (based on 260 working days, five-day week).

For example:

ITEM	FIRST YEAR	SECOND YEAR
Daily earning	$ 131.00	$ 131.00
Weekly earnings	$ 655.00	$ 655.00
Monthly earnings	$ 2,836.00	$ 2,836.00
Yearly earnings	$34,032.00	$34,032.00

Keep in mind that a master plan must be practical, challenging, and within the scope of reality. Unless you can meet each goal within a reasonable amount of time, it has little value.

4. Closely monitor your progress

Having good intentions and spelling them out on paper are two giant steps in a big thinker's climb to the top. A third, critical step involves checking your progress and making sure everything stays on schedule.

Study the following example of weekly earnings. This salesperson's big-thinking objective is to earn $30,000 during the current year. Therefore the salesperson will have to earn approximately $115.40 per day, or $577 a week.

DAY	WEEK ONE	WEEK TWO	WEEK THREE
M	$ 90.00	$ 73.00	$ 65.00
Tu	$110.00	$ 98.00	$ 72.00
W	$ 86.50	$123.00	$106.50
Th	$180.00	$108.00	$ 98.50
F	$130.00	$172.00	$100.00
TOTAL	$596.50	$574.00	$442.00

A close examination reveals the following information:

- Monday and Tuesday are low-producing days.
- The salesperson lags behind after three weeks by $118.50.

- The salesperson will have to earn $696 in the fourth week to stay on schedule.
- The salesperson's earnings have steadily nosedived since the first week.
- The salesperson earned $115.40 or more per day only four days! Translation: This person operates at 26 percent efficiency.

Tracking, then, does six things: 1) it helps you stay on schedule; 2) it pinpoints strengths and weaknesses in your selling progress; 3) it keeps you alert, active, and well informed; 4) it gives you a daily progress report; 5) it helps you improve your organizational skills; and 6) it paves the way for big-thinking results.

LIVING YOUR GOALS

So far you've established a big-thinking objective and recorded your intentions for reaching your major goal. Now you must live your goals to keep them alive and well.

How do you live your goals? Simply by continually thinking and living big. You can do this by:

1. Not allowing small things to get in your way.
2. Looking at your selling territory as an orchard loaded with plump, ripe fruit.
3. Placing no limits or restrictions on yourself.
4. Radiating confidence in everything you do.
5. Looking at each new day as an exciting challenge that brings you closer to your major goal.
6. Looking at selling as the most important thing you'll ever do.
7. Cooperating and sharing ideas with those around you.
8. Expecting big things of yourself and your environment.
9. Working hard until you reach your big-thinking objective.
10. Making things happen—*now*.

POINTS TO REMEMBER

In this chapter you have seen how a big-thinking salesperson is a dedicated individual with an insatiable thirst to achieve success. A big thinker combines the magic of desire, determination, dedication, and discipline. A big thinker relies on a success formula based on intelligent programming.

A big thinker creates a Master Plan for action by setting realistic goals and expending a maximal effort to reach these goals within a reasonable length of time.

A big thinker breathes life into each goal and prevents negative forces from setting up roadblocks by developing a strong, positive attitude.

CHAPTER TWO

THE MAGIC OF SETTING THE STAGE FOR BIG SALES

Sure, you're a good salesperson. But as a big thinker, good isn't enough. You want more—more prospects, more sales, and of course, more earnings. How do you set the stage for higher earnings? By activating a five-step plan. This plan includes the following:

1. Preparing yourself to sell big
2. Analyzing the selling scene
3. Evaluating yourself as a big-thinking salesperson
4. Turning your self-evaluation into big earnings
5. Powerizing your total selling package

Let's see how each of these steps provides the magic for setting the stage for big sales.

1. PREPARING YOURSELF TO SELL BIG

Selling is acting and acting is selling. A salesperson, like an actor, must control the selling scene. For example, take the film *Coming Home* with Jane Fonda and Jon Voight. How many people do you think left their seats during the performance to buy popcorn or candy? Chances are very few did. Why? Simply because these two talented actors had full control of every scene, feeding the viewers' senses with enough stimuli to take their minds off food. That's control. That's exceptional acting.

You must do the same thing with a prospect. You must control every aspect of the selling scene. Controlling an acting scene and controlling a selling situation are synonymous. They both require concentration, hard work, and sound preparation. A serious actor wouldn't go on stage unprepared any more than a salesperson would waste time selling a nonexistent product.

How many times, as a salesperson, do you think about the performance you are going to give? In other words, how often do you rehearse a selling scene? You see, many experienced salespeople make the same mistake; they sell a product or service in the same way to nearly every prospect. In time, they reach a plateau and remain there. Unfortunately, in these instances salespeople become disillusioned with selling and seek a more lucrative way of earning a living.

Why don't these salespeople succeed? Why do they quit after three or four years? Because they lack the insight to adjust to the special needs of prospects. Therefore, preparing yourself to sell big requires a complete, honest appraisal of your sales presentation each time you meet a new prospect.

Think back to those selling days when beads of perspiration sprinted down the bridge of your nose like downhill racers. Remember those nerve-racking hours you spent stumbling through your presentation? Those tiny hammers in your brain pounded a familiar tune ... "keep working until you get it right."

Well, now you've got it right. The only problem is that satisfaction may encourage you to accept mediocre results when superlative results are within your grasp. Never, never allow satisfaction to get in the way of success. Sometimes those cerebral hammers lie. They signal that once a presentation begins to flow smoothly there's no reason to worry. Burn that message right now. Gather the ashes and bury them forever. Remember, contentment kills in the selling game. Christian Nestell Bovee said it best: "One who is contented with what he has done will never become famous for what he will do. He has lain down to die, and the grass is already over him."

As a big thinker, you can prepare yourself to sell big by employing the following suggestions:

1. Tag line the strong points of your presentation. In other words, single out those items that give your sales presentation punch. In the back of your appointment book list the key points that consistently hook the prospect, then find a common denominator. Here's an example:

SELLING PRODUCT OR SERVICE: *NEWSPAPER ADVERTISING*

STRONG POINTS	COMMON DENOMINATOR
• Product offers *quality* and *dependable* service.	
• Product offers an *inexpensive* way to advertise.	Product will allow prospect to advertise within budget
• Product offers a service *comparable with competing firms*.	limitations and increase sales.

Now underline or circle the word or words in the tag line that pack the power. Notice how these words accentuate the positive and keep the presentation moving forward at a fast pace.

As satisfactory as this model appears, it would be unwise to use the same presentation with tag lines for every prospect because each prospect carries a special set of needs.

2. If possible, ascertain in advance the special needs of a prospect. Then adjust your sales presentation accordingly.

3. Dress up your sales presentation. Treat it like a personal resumé by bringing it up to date and filling in the rough spots with fresh ideas.

4. Listen to the advice of others. If you hear or see something you like, give it a try.

How effective your sales presentation will be depends upon your determination to become a big-thinking salesperson. Let's face it. You're in the selling game to earn money—big money. So once your selling plan gathers momentum, you're on your way.

For example, take the case of Bill Edwards, salesman for a national copy products company. Last year he struggled to earn $13,000. He experienced difficulty talking with professional people and confessed a certain uneasiness when demonstrating his product.

Bill attended one of my in-house sales workshops held in Sacramento, California. After the workshop he approached me and asked for help. I explained how tag lining would strengthen his sales presentation and make him more aware of a prospect's needs. Bill agreed to try this technique and let me know the results.

It worked. Six months later Bill called me and said the technique gave him a new awareness which, in turn, provided the confidence he needed to push for higher sales. Bill expects to nearly double his earnings by the end of the year.

2. ANALYZING THE SELLING SCENE

A big-thinking salesperson, like a psychologist, studies people and learns to anticipate how a prospect will react under certain conditions. This almost seems too basic to even mention, yet enough salespeople score an F on their selling scorecard to create concern.

As an example, the following test will give you an idea of how well you analyze a selling situation. Be honest. Mentally select an answer for each response.

1. You smile; a prospect _____ .

2. A prospect talks; you _____ .

3. You laugh and feel cheerful; a prospect _____ .

4. You emit enthusiasm; a prospect _____ .

5. You speak in a casual, relaxed manner; a prospect _____ .

6. You take a genuine interest in the prospect; a prospect reciprocates by _____ .

7. You enjoy selling; a prospect _____ .

The ideal answers, of course, are:

1. smiles.
2. listen attentively.
3. responds in a lively manner.
4. becomes enthusiastic.
5. remains calm and at ease.

6. believing in you and your product or service.

7. enjoys buying.

If you're following a big thinker's success formula, chances are your answers either hit the target or landed near the bullseye. As you know, selling is a people business. Part of the magic of setting the stage for big sales comes from knowing people and being able to predict with accuracy how they will respond to specific stimuli. Therefore, here's a five-point approach to help you personalize your way to higher earnings:

1. People like to talk about themselves. Since prospects are people, encourage them to do so. Be an active listener.

2. Enjoy laughing. Have a good time. Let the prospect know you're in a satisfying profession and enjoy what you do.

3. Apply a personal touch in everything you do. Let a prospect know how much you really care.

4. Promote a friendly atmosphere by centering your sales presentation around your prospect's need, not what you think the prospect should have.

5. Use all of your senses to make sound judgments.

3. EVALUATING YOURSELF AS A BIG-THINKING SALESPERSON

As a big thinker, you must evaluate your progress continually and make an honest appraisal of your selling performance. A self-evaluation is like tuning up your car. If you service the moving parts, the parts will keep moving.

What "moving parts" comprise a big thinker's sales package? As mentioned earlier, they are the Four *D*'s: desire, determination, dedication, and discipline. Under each "moving part" ask yourself these questions:

DESIRE

1. Does your presentation move at a brisk pace?

2. Have you made total commitment to succeed?

3. Do you believe wholeheartedly in what you are trying to accomplish?

4. Are you constantly seeking ways to improve your presentation?

DETERMINATION

1. Do you immerse yourself completely into the selling scene, but set your goals within the scope of reality?
2. Do you apply a *do it now* philosophy?
3. Do you always sell with a positive mental attitude?
4. Do you stick with your game plan but keep your eyes open for a better way of doing things?

DEDICATION

1. Do you demand a 100-percent effort from yourself at all times?
2. Do you implement fresh, updated ideas that add zest to your selling profession?
3. Do you interact with others and share their experiences?
4. Do you inject a happy spirit into everything you do?

DISCIPLINE

1. Do you write down your goals?
2. Do you work extra hard to meet your goals?
3. Do you prepare yourself for meeting the daily challenge of selling? In other words, do you list each day's activities and how you plan to complete each task?
4. Are you willing to improvise or change your plans if things go awry?

Each "yes" answer brings you one step closer to your ultimate goal of doubling or tripling your income. Now let's examine a two-part plan for evaluating your success as a big-thinking salesperson.

Self-Analysis Checklist

After giving a sales presentation treat yourself to a series of instant replays by mentally picturing the selling stage. Go over each scene, act by act. You can do this while walking about, drinking a cup of coffee, or driving your car to your next appointment. Think about the flow of conversation and ask yourself such questions as these: Was I in full control at all times? Was I enthusiastic? Was I relaxed? And so on.

The best way to find out is by recording your answers on a self-analysis checklist sheet. You must respond to each question immediately following your presentation, while the information is still fresh in your mind.

Type the following guidelines on a sheet of paper. Then duplicate enough copies to last for several weeks.

SELF-ANALYSIS CHECKLIST

Name of business or service _____   Prospect's name _____

_____

Sale _____   No sale _____

A. Check the weakest part of your selling plan during this presentation:

    1. Cold call _____

    2. Describing the prospect _____

    3. Front talk _____

    4. The presentation itself _____

    5. Answering questions _____

    6. Handling objections _____

    7. Closing the sale _____

    8. Getting leads from the prospect _____

B. How would you describe this prospect?

    1. Good-natured _____

    2. Open-minded _____

    3. Apathetic _____

    4. Egotistical _____

    5. Curious _____

    6. Know it all _____

    7. Religious _____

    8. Angry _____

    9. Enthusiastic _____

   10. Timid _____

   11. Skeptical _____

   12. Procrastinator _____

   13. Cautious _____

   14. Cynical _____

C. Cold Calling
1. Did you neutralize the prospect's mind? _____

2. Did you get the prospect to feel comfortable? _____

3. Did you get the prospect to talk? _____

4. In your opinion, did the prospect like you? _____

5. Did the prospect want to see your product or service?
_____

6. Did you show your product or service to the prospect immediately? _____

D. Front Talk
1. Was the prospect tense? _____

2. Was the prospect relaxed? _____

3. Did the conversation flow smoothly? _____

4. Was the conversation forced? _____

5. Who dominated the conversation, you or the prospect?
_____

6. Who asked the questions, you or the prospect? _____

7. In general, did the talk go well? _____

8. Did you find out what the prospect wanted or needed?
_____

E. Presenting the Proposition
   1. Did you create an aura of excitement in your presentation? _____

   2. Did you present your proposition in a professional manner? _____

   3. Did you give an enthusiastic presentation? _____
   4. Did the prospect ask intelligent questions? _____
   5. Did you answer the questions intelligently? _____
   6. Did you immediately convince the prospect that he needed your product or service? _____
   7. If you answered "no" to Question 6, what do you think went wrong? _____
   8. On a scale of 1 (poor) to 10 (outstanding) grade your presentation. _____

F. Handling Questions and Objections
   1. Did the prospect ask many questions? _____
   2. List the two most important questions your prospect asked:
      (a) _____
      (b) _____
   3. Did you answer these questions with confidence? _____ Without much confidence? _____ In a matter-of-fact fashion? _____
   4. Briefly list the prospect's main objections to your presentation or product or service. _____
      _____
      _____
   5. Would you consider these main objections of prime importance? _____
   6. Did any objections throw off your sales presentation? _____
   7. If so, how did you handle the situation? _____
      _____
   8. Did you reverse any objection into a positive reason for buying? _____

9. If so, how did you do it? _____

_____

G. Describing the Prospect
   1. Whom did you talk with? Owner? _____ Part-
      ner? _____ Wife? _____ Husband? _____
      Other? _____

   2. How did the prospect's business/home appear? Immaculate?
      _____ Neat? _____ Sloppy? _____

   3. How did the prospect's business/home appear financially?
      Prosperous? _____   Average? _____
      Poor? _____

   4. Did you feel that the prospect could afford your product/
      service? _____

   5. Did you find out what product or service the prospect is
      presently using? _____

   6. Did you find out what your prospect likes most about his
      present product or service? _____

   7. Did you find out what he dislikes most about his present
      product or service? _____

   8. Will he continue using present product or service? _____

H. Closing the Sale
   1. Did the prospect buy your product or service? _____

   2. If "yes," did the sale come early in the presentation?
      _____

   3. Was the sale a relatively easy one? _____

   4. If you didn't clinch the sale, why do you think the prospect
      didn't buy? _____

      _____

   5. How many trial closes did you make? _____ How did
      the prospect respond to these closes? _____

      _____

   6. After testing the sales climate with trial closes, how many
      times did you attempt to close? _____

7. At the end of each close did you carefully observe your prospect's reactions? _____

8. After your first close what did the prospect say and how did he react? The prospect said _____

_____

The prospect reacted by _____

_____

9. How much pressure or tension was present during the close? _____

10. What did you do to ease the situation? _____

_____

11. How do you honestly feel about your close? _____

_____

I. Getting Leads from the Prospects
   1. Did you ask the prospect for leads? _____ If so, how many did you get? _____

   2. Do you feel you have a successful approach for acquiring leads? _____

   3. How do you think you can improve your skills in acquiring leads? _____

   _____

ANALYSIS SUMMARY OF THE SALES PRESENTATION

_____

_____

_____

_____

Again, keeping accurate records by writing things down for ready reference is the big thinker's key to pinpointing strengths and weaknesses in each sales presentation. Unfortunately, it takes persistence and patience to overshadow the monotonous task of steady recording. But there's no better way to break down a presentation and study each component part. Later chapters will expand on the selling steps listed in the self-analysis checklist.

Weekly Tally Cards

Pinpoint the weak spots in your sales presentation by recording them on a summary tally card, one card per selling step, for the entire week.

You'll need seven 3 by 5 or 5 by 7 cards. Here are the seven selling steps:

1. Cold calling
2. Front talk
3. Presenting the proposition
4. Handling questions and objections
5. Qualifying the prospect
6. Closing the sale
7. Getting leads from the prospect

On the front side of each card include the following information: week number, days, selling step, and related problems.

A typical example is shown in Figure 2-1.

Figure 2-1

SELF-ANALYSIS CHECKLIST
WEEKLY TALLY CARD

Week Number: _____0_____ From: _____3/7_____ To: ___3/11_____

Closing the Sale
32 presentations—14 sales; 18 no sales.

Problems
1. Spending too much time on trial closes.
2. Having tendency to press or push sale onto prospect.
3. Need to be more attentive to prospect's mood.

Turn the card over and write in bold letters REMEDIATION. Then outline your strategy for corrective action. An example is shown in Figure 2-2.

Figure 2-2

REMEDIATION

1. Tighten presentation, get to the point, and be more assertive.
2. Listen to prospect, sympathize with present needs, then close with style.
3. Open up senses, really *listen* to front talk. Stay flexible and adjust presentation accordingly.

Keep these cards and the self-analysis sheet in a manila envelope with the date (five-day time period) marked on the outside. Place the envelope in a drawer, shelf, or file cabinet for safekeeping. Remember, this material is meaningless unless you use the information to help you become a topnotch, big-thinking salesperson.

This two-step, self-analysis plan produces outstanding results when conscientiously applied. For instance, Beverly Randal, a salesperson from San Diego, threatened to quit the selling profession following three low-producing years. For the next two years she kept accurate notes by recording the highlights of her sales presentations, especially the problem areas.

She concentrated on strengthening these weak spots through mental rehearsal following each presentation. She sought advice from others. She wrote everything down, weeded out the extraneous material, and set her sights for bigger sales. Within two years her sales volume increased and her earnings from the previous year climbed from $13,500 to $28,000.

4. TURNING YOUR SELF-EVALUATION INTO BIG EARNINGS

Another layer of magic spreads over the selling scene when you *record* the actual number of calls you make, rather than guess as you go along. This daily scorecard (Figure 2-3) includes the number of cold calls, appointments, call backs, presentations, sales, and no sales.

Figure 2-3

Items	DAILY SCORECARD					
	M	**Tu**	**W**	**Th**	**F**	**Total**
Cold Calls	ЖЖ ЖЖ ЖЖ III	ЖЖ IIII	III	ЖЖ ЖЖ ЖЖ ЖЖ II		*52*
Appointments	III	ЖЖ	I	ЖЖ III	ЖЖ	*22*
Call Backs	IIII	II	I	III	II	*12*
Presentations	II	ЖЖ	I	II	ЖЖ I	*16*
Sales	II	III		II	IIII	*11*
No Sales		II	I		II	*5*

After each contact mark the appropriate column by putting a tally mark in the proper space. At the end of the week total the tally marks. This gives you a clear picture of your selling progress during the week. Keep your clipboard next to you as you call on new prospects. Make it a daily habit to check your records. Keeping daily records throws a roadblock in front of Mr. Negative and prevents him from sabotaging your selling contacts.

The negative voice specializes in exaggerating the actual number of calls you make. As an example, when you make one call, the negative voice tells you that you've made two. Then when you make two, Mr. Negative whispers four, and so on. The negative voice fools even the most experienced salesperson. By keeping daily records, then, you nail the the lid down tightly on Mr. Negative.

Remember, a "no" response following a sales presentation has a way of making the day drag on. Also, you must know *exactly* how many calls you need to make a year and how many sales to clinch before you can reach your big-thinking objective, which is to double or triple your income.

Before moving on let's review the big-thinking strategy covered in this chapter so far. These are the major points:

1. Prepare yourself mentally and physically to sell.
2. Dissect your presentation and study the integral parts. Tag line the *strong points*. Know what you are doing right.

3. Personalize your selling approach.

4. Build your sales program around the four *D*s of selling success: desire, determination, dedication, and discipline.

5. Test the effectiveness of your sales presentation by setting up a self-analysis checklist for each prospect.

6. Prepare weekly tally cards from your sales presentations to isolate and correct the troublesome areas.

7. Stay on target by keeping a daily scorecard. The scorecard lets you know *exactly* how many calls you make, plus sales, and gives you firsthand information regarding your progress in reaching your established goals.

How can a daily scorecard double or triple your income? Let's say you are selling television advertising and your goal is to triple your income over a 12-month period—$75,000. You're now making $25,000 a year.

Simple mathematics suggest that you will have to make $6,250 a month in order to reach your goal. Also, you know that it takes sales of about $21,600 per month to earn your monthly pay, which is based on a salary and commission package.

Last year, for instance, your best-selling week (March 26-30) looked like the example shown in Figure 2-4.

Figure 2-4

Items	M	Tu	W	Th	F	Total
	DAILY SCORECARD					
Cold Calls	ﬀﬀ ﬀﬀﬀ ﬀﬀﬀﬀﬀ ﬀﬀﬀ	ﬀﬀﬀ ﬀﬀﬀﬀ	ﬀﬀ ﬀﬀﬀ //	ﬀﬀﬀ ﬀﬀﬀ	ﬀﬀﬀ ///	70
Appointments	ﬀﬀﬀ	ﬀﬀﬀ //	ﬀﬀﬀ ﬀﬀﬀ	ﬀﬀﬀ ﬀﬀﬀ	//	34
Call Backs	////	//	//	////	/	13
Presentations	ﬀﬀﬀ ﬀﬀﬀ	///	ﬀﬀﬀ	ﬀﬀﬀ /	//	26
Sales	////	//	//	//	/	11
No Sales	ﬀﬀﬀ /	////	//	//	/	15

Weekly Earnings $= \$1,500.00$

You would have to *equal* the selling success of your *best* week every week for approximately 50 weeks in order to triple your income. Therefore, a critical day-to-day examination of everything that transpired from March 26 through March 30 should reveal the factors that combine to form the ideal selling climate for increasing your income threefold.

Your self-check might include such suggestions as these:

1. What specific things did I do on Monday that made it the most productive day (most sales) of the week?
2. In what way were my presentations more effective during this time period?
3. Why were the prospects more receptive to buying my product or service during this time period?
4. What specific things must I consistently do in order to triple my earnings?
5. How can I prepare myself to think big *every* week?

How can you use your daily scorecard to reach big-thinking goals?

Let's say you sell a paper product, and on the average each order hovers around $110. Your daily goal is to place six orders or sell approximately $660 worth of supplies. You can use your daily scorecard to help you reach your goal in the following way:

1. Begin by opening your appointment book to Monday of next week. On a separate sheet of paper write APPOINTMENT LIST and DATE at the top of the page. Then make four columns with these labels: Time, Place of Business, Person to Contact, and Comments (Figure 2-5).

In order to reach your daily goal you'll have to sell at least $110 worth of paper products to six customers. Of course some customers buy more than others so you'll have to adjust your selling plan accordingly. As a big thinker, however, the more sales you make, the sooner you'll reach your goal and be in an excellent position to go for higher stakes. A big-thinking salesperson uses a daily goal as a guideline, not as a stopping point.

Figure 2-5

APPOINTMENT LIST
October 6, Monday

Time	Place of Business	Person to Contact	Comments
8 A.M.	Zell's Variety Store	B. Johns	Cagey, handle with care
9:15 A.M.	Country Square	L. Layne	Nice person, funny
10 A.M.	Suburban Faire	J. Vanderson	Quiet person
11 A.M.	Joseph's Department Store	A. Nuney	Hard-nosed, not too friendly
Noon	Kelly's Korner	M. Davis	Easy-going, likeable
1 P.M.	Lanston's	C. Doyle	Cautious type, rough to sell
2 P.M.	Circle Center	K. Franklin	Nice guy, very pleasant
3:30 P.M.	Loude's Supplies	B. Grande	Don't know very well
4:15 P.M.	Valley View	E. J. Silver	Tough person to handle
5:30 P.M.	Imperial Place	T. Ames	Have seen only once

2. Each time you take an order for $110 or more, lightly draw a line through the contact's name and place of business. If for some reason you fail to meet a contact, place a check mark in the Person to Contact space on the appointment list. Reschedule the appointment for the following day if possible. The main thing is to reschedule immediately. If you don't, you'll lose track. And once that happens confusion sets in and Mr. Negative takes over.

The appointment list record acts as a roadmap and guides you through a busy day. It provides you with an accurate sales record and offers a handy reminder regarding the disposition or attitude of your contacts.

5. POWERIZING YOUR TOTAL SELLING PACKAGE

Positive results come from an action-oriented selling program laced with immediate and long-range goals. The magic arrives when you tailor each working day to match your needs, ability, and determination to keep moving at a brisk pace. This entire selling plan draws its first breath the moment you transform yourself into a big-thinking salesperson.

How then can you powerize your selling package and double or triple your earnings? Here are six suggestions:

1. Establish a daily plan of action. Write out everything you want to accomplish each day. Never trust anything to memory. Once you write out your strategy you've made a commitment to yourself and feel compelled to carry out your plan.

2. Put your plan to immediate use. Stay on schedule and don't let anything or anyone stop you from reaching your daily goals.

3. Stay self-motivated by looking at each appointment and presentation as a personal challenge. Keeping an active scorecard and checking it constantly serves as a powerful self-motivating device.

4. Use your daily scorecard to uncover weaknesses in your sales presentations. Each time you isolate and remove a weakness your presentation gains strength and takes you one giant step closer to your goal.

5. By keeping accurate records and daily scorecards, your selling plan parallels a competitive sporting event. For example, in order to win and reach your big-thinking goal, you must be strong, determined, and have an insatiable thirst for winning.

6. Devise a selling program that works best for you. Use the previous suggestions to help you mold a system commensurate with your individual selling style.

POINTS TO REMEMBER

The success of your big-thinking selling plan revolves around your desire, determination, dedication, and discipline to be the best salesperson possible.

You'll need to critically examine your daily progress and expose your weaknesses and strengths. Only by removing the weak spots and powerizing your strengths will you reach your big-thinking objective. A thorough examination of self-analysis checklists, weekly tally cards, and daily scorecards lets you know exactly how you are doing at any given time.

Your ability to reach your established goals hinges on keeping accurate records and evaluating the results. You must constantly seek improvement and allow nothing to stand in your way.

CHAPTER THREE

COLD CALLING
MAGIC
IN ACTION

You know the importance of injecting self-confidence into everything you do. Nobody has to point out to you how a strong, positive approach builds large bank accounts in the selling profession. As a big-thinking salesperson you welcome any challenge that tests your ability to sell, sell, sell.

So prepare yourself for perhaps the biggest challenge of them all: cold calling.

ANALYZING THE MENTAL SIDE OF COLD CALLING

Few salespeople would deny that an effective cold caller earns big money in selling. Yet many salespeople either take cold calling for granted or simply minimize the number of contacts they make. Ask yourself these questions:

1. If cold calling is so important, why do many salespeople shy away from making them?
2. Why don't companies and agencies devote more time to training their salespeople in making cold calls?
3. Why do many salespeople consider cold calling demeaning?

First, many salespeople feel uneasy making cold calls because they are never quite sure how a prospect will respond to them. Therefore it becomes increasingly difficult to approach an unknown situation with enthusiasm. Second, a substantial number of companies feel that their salespeople are reluctant to make cold calls. They are hesitant to force an unpopular idea on their salespeople. Third, many salespeople regard any uncomfortable situation that casts doubts upon their ability to communicate as demoralizing. Thus, cold calling creates an uneasy atmosphere rife with negative overtones.

What actually happens when you make a cold call? Well, the moment you come face to face with a prospect several things occur. Your mental wheels begin to spin. They churn out ideas that bounce around inside of your head like a ping pong ball trapped in a wind tunnel. Imagine two mental forces emerging and taking shape. Let's call the first force Mr. Positive and the second force Mr. Negative. How you respond to these voices determines your success at mastering cold calls.

By listening and following Mr. Positive's advice, you'll score big sales—over and over again. In Chapter 2 you read how Mr. Negative lies and deliberately creates total confusion. Mr. Negative takes great pride in planting the seed of self-doubt.

The two voices continually contradict each other. Let's say, for example, that you are making a cold call on a prospect who runs a small business on the south side of town. The inner conversation might go something like this:

POSITIVE VOICE: I'm going to schedule at least eight presentations today.

NEGATIVE VOICE: Say, let's get out of here. This old, rundown building looks bad.

POSITIVE VOICE: My product fits in well here. This location has great possibilities.

NEGATIVE VOICE: Forget it. It's a waste of time.

Simple arithmetic tells you that two positives and two negatives cancel each other when you allow them to clash. You wind up in a standoff. And a standoff, like a stalemate in chess, ends in a draw. Nobody wins. No win equals no success. Period.

In order to rate as a big-thinking salesperson you must wipe out negative thoughts and allow Mr. Positive to gain full control. This, of course, requires concentration and perseverance. With Mr. Positive in command you slip into the role of detective and sleuth about for qualified prospects. Even the best salesperson in the world can't sell everyone. Therefore you look for only those prospects who *need* and *can afford* your product or service.

How does a wise salesperson make prospects aware of their needs? Here are three ways.

First, ask intelligent questions that reveal a prospect's attitude, economic situation, present plans, or long-range goals. If you ask questions requiring more than a yes or no answer from a prospect, three things are likely to occur: 1) you'll stay in control of the conversation; 2) the prospect opens up and speaks freely; and 3) a friendship bond develops between you and the prospect.

Second, listen carefully to what the prospect says. Then paraphrase the prospect's remarks by stating in your own way what you hear. You can do this by trying to put the prospect's statement into your own words. For example:

> YOU: Mr. Casey, it looks like you've put a lot of work into this business. How long have you been here?
>
> MR. CASEY: We've been here three years. And, yes, there have been
> (PROSPECT) plenty of tough obstacles to overcome. In fact, we're still hard at it.
>
> YOU: Well, I hope all that hard work pays off for you. Anyone expending so much effort should be rewarded accordingly.

This technique shows the prospect that you're an active listener with a common interest—the prospect's welfare.

Third, make it easy for the prospect to say yes by demonstrating exactly how your product or service meets your prospect's needs, including a feasible way for the prospect to pay for the product or service.

Is there a big-thinker's action plan for making successful cold calls? Yes, and here it is:

1. As mentioned earlier, you strengthen your selling machine by establishing and reaching attainable goals and objectives. Thus, a major objective should be to consider *each* cold-call situation as a nonthreatening, personal challenge that provides for building positive selling skills. This approach requires you to do three things. They are:

  - Anticipate a future sale. Make your cold call presentation better than the previous one.

Figure 3-1

COLD CALL COMMITMENT PLAN OF ACTION

My strong points	What I need to work on	Plan of improvement	How will plan be implemented?	Evidence of success
Like to meet new prospects.	Be more convincing with my cold-calling approach.	Address presentation to specific needs of prospects.	1. By listening attentively. 2. By asking intelligent questions. 3. By putting self in prospect's position.	Check to see if cold calls lead to successful sales.
Give enthusiastic presentations.	Not to be too eager or too quick to schedule sales presentations.	Pace cold call presentation to current interest of prospect.	1. By "getting to know" prospect before trying to make a big sale. 2. By stressing the importance of small talk.	Check to see if cold calls lead to successful sales.

Remember, the magic of any big thinker's plan comes when the plan springs into immediate action. *Do it now!*

- Treat every prospect as an excellent opportunity for you to demonstrate your big-thinking ability to communicate.
- Firmly believe that you can call on anyone at any time—and set the stage for a future sale.

2. Tag line your cold-calling strong points. Record on a chart what you do well and what needs to be done for further improvement. Then make a commitment to action. Your recording chart might look like Figure 3-1.

3. Graph and chart your daily cold call results. Examples of a graph and chart are shown in Figures 3-2 and 3-3.

Figure 3-2

COLD CALLS VS. SCHEDULED SALES PRESENTATION GRAPH
(Week of November 12-16)

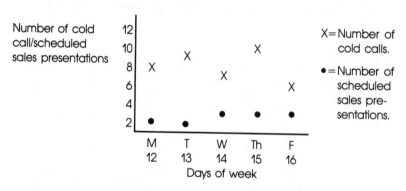

Figure 3-3

DATA CHART FOR WEEK OF NOVEMBER 12-16						
Days	**M**	**Tu**	**W**	**Th**	**F**	**Total**
Number of cold calls	8	9	7	10	6	40
Number of scheduled sales presentations	2	2	3	3	3	13
Sales success percentage	25	22	43	30	50	34

By graphing your ratio of cold calls to scheduled sales presentations on a weekly basis, several items come to your attention. They are:

1. The actual number of cold calls you make each day or week.

2. The actual number of scheduled sales presentations you make each day or week.

3. Your scheduled sales presentations on a daily or weekly basis.

4. The ratio between cold calls and scheduled sales presentations on a daily or weekly basis.

5. An indication of which days are the most productive for you. You might discover, for instance, that you schedule more sales presentations on Wednesday and Friday than on any other day. Find out why these particular days seem to work best for you. Then try hard to turn every selling day into Wednesday and Friday.

6. An opportunity to see immediate results. See, for example, the graphs in Figure 3-4.

Figure 3-4

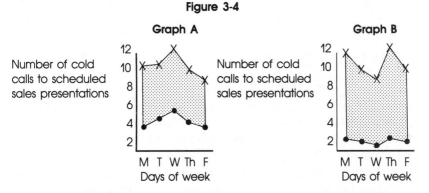

Which graph shows the highest yield for the week? Graph A, of course. The shaded zone illustrates the relationship between number of cold calls and number of scheduled presentations. You immediately see that a small shaded area indicates a higher number of scheduled sales presentations.

4. You must develop an "I've got to make this cold call *now*" attitude. To ask yourself, "Should I make this cold call?" opens the door for doubt, confusion, and procrastination.

As a big-thinking salesperson you can double or triple your earnings by using cold calling as a vehicle for seeking out qualified prospects. In fact, if you diagram the relationship, it would look like Figure 3-5.

Figure 3-5

In summary, you can make big money in sales if you meet and accept the challenge of cold calling without feeling put upon or debased. With few exceptions, a big-thinking salesperson is also a master cold caller. A big thinker gives first-rate presentations, seeks qualified prospects through cold calling, and keeps an updated log showing the relationship between cold calling and scheduled sales presentations.

HOW MUCH DOES APPEARANCE COUNT?

As a professional salesperson you know the importance of good, conservative grooming. And unless you are attending a Halloween party, you wouldn't be wearing loud, flashy clothing when calling on a prospect. Without question, clothing should aid, not hinder, a sale.

A big-thinking salesperson knows the value of personal appearance, especially when making cold calls. This appearance, in most instances, sets the mood and pace for the entire selling scenario. In other words, appearance counts. Your appearance means everything to a prospect who spend no more than two seconds sizing you up.

Did you know that an average prospect forms an impression of you in just two seconds? That's right—one thousand one, one thousand two—two seconds. And the real clincher comes from a prospect who doesn't bother counting because he already has a preformed notion that all salespeople are tricky, pushy, and dishonest. To this prospect, all salespeople wear suits and carry briefcases.

Unless your company compels you to wear a suit, use your own discretion on what to wear and when to wear it. And that goes for the briefcase too. If you don't need to carry one, leave it at home or in the back seat of your car.

If you dress casually, the prospect who specializes in stereotyping people won't know who you are or what you want, right? You're in full control and can win this prospect over before he has time to form nasty thoughts about you. This isn't subterfuge, just a simple appeal to your common sense: Wear attire that will aid, not impede.

A COLD CALLER'S CHECKLIST

How do you really feel about making cold calls? There's a way for you to find out. Grab a pencil and sheet of paper. Number one through eight on the left-hand side of the paper, and make a yes and a no column on the right-hand side of the paper.

Now read each statement in the following Cold Caller's Checklist and mark either the yes or the no column.

COLD CALLER'S CHECKLIST

1. I believe what Mark Twain once said: "Honesty is the best policy—when there is money in it."

2. When I approach a prospect my only concern is to sell my product or service.

3. It's vitally important that I do most of the talking in order to schedule a sales presentation.

4. If I memorize my cold call presentation, I'll increase my chances of scheduling a sales presentation.

5. Engaging in small talk wastes time for me and my prospect.

6. My "power position" with a prospect comes from talking, not listening.

7. My cold-calling approach should be the same with every prospect; too much flexibility invites confusion.

8. I can establish a strong rapport with a prospect almost immediately.

If you checked yes on one or more of the items, read the next section carefully. If you checked no on every item, treat yourself to an extra helping of cold calling confidence. Then read on.

EIGHT BIG-THINKING STEPS TO MASTERING COLD CALLING

A piece of cold calling magic appears when you win a friend and gain a sale. A sound, practical cold calling approach thrives in an atmosphere of mutual trust. As an experienced salesperson you know it takes more than grins and handshakes to pay the rent. And the big payoff arrives when you mold your cold calling approach to match the needs and interests of your prospect.

How can you be sure you are reaching the prospect during the cold call? Here are eight ways:

1. By neutralizing the prospect's mind
2. By establishing a solid customer rapport
3. By maintaining flexibility at all times
4. By getting the prospect to feel comfortable
5. By getting the prospect to talk
6. By getting the prospect to like you
7. By getting the prospect to want to see your product or service
8. By establishing a power position during conversation

Let's see how each of these eight points will help you to acquire qualified prospects and bring you a giant step closer to doubling or tripling your earnings.

1. Neutralizing the prospect's mind

When you meet a prospect for the first time it's difficult to know exactly what to say or do. Relying on a canned presentation invites disaster; so does an overly cautious or aggressive approach. An overly cautious presentation build tension and puts the prospect on edge. Conversely, if you come on too strong, a prospect loses patience and slams the door on communication. These methods work against you because both of them spawn negative impressions in the prospect's mind.

The ideal situation would be to start your presentation in a low-key, nonchalant manner. This keeps a prospect from becoming anxious and forming instant negative images of you. It's best to deal with a prospect who doesn't develop an immediate negative or positive view. This neutralization process gives you a fertile, open mind to work with. What happens next is directly proportional to your knowledge of people and your ability to apply a big-thinker's action plan.

2. Establishing a solid customer rapport

A harmonious relationship begins when your words and actions blend with the needs and desires of a prospect. In most cold-call situations a prospect will react as you do. If, for instance, you appear jumpy and tense, chances are your prospect will feel uneasy too. Conversely, a hearty handshake with a friendly smile signals a prospect that you are okay.

How can you show genuine interest in a prospect? By keeping your eyes open for anything that your prospect seems to hold in high regard. It may be a bowling trophy or a golfing trophy or a stuffed deer head or an unusual painting or perhaps a framed certificate hanging on the wall.

As an example, let's say you enter the office of Jack Coleman, District Manager of Guthrie Electronics. You notice a tall, shiny golfing trophy resting on a bookcase next to his desk. You shake Mr. Coleman's hand, introduce yourself, and begin the front talk that sets your cold-calling wheels in motion. The conversation might go something like this:

YOU: (pointing to the trophy) I see you're a golfer, Mr. Coleman.

MR. C: Yes, but I don't have chance to play much.

YOU: What's your handicap?

MR. C: Oh, about ... 11.

YOU: How often do you play?

MR. C: About once every two weeks.

YOU: Mr. Coleman, I play once a week and I shoot to an 18. Now either I'm awfully bad or you're awfully good, or one of us is pulling the other's leg.
(Both laugh)

YOU: Remind me never to play you for money, okay?

MR. C: No, really, I'm not that good!

YOU: Well, neither am I.
(Both laugh again)

How long the conversation lasts depends on the length of time the prospect remains interested in the subject matter. That's why it's critical that the front talk remain casual, interesting, and pointed directly at the prospect.

You've started a good conversation. Notice how Mr. Coleman isn't setting up defenses. He doesn't have to because there is no reason for it. Sure, he's a busy man, but you are talking about his interests, not your new sailboat or your product or service.

Mr. Coleman's no fool. He knows you are there to interest him in your product or service. However, he enjoys golf and appreciates your interest in his achievements. Treating a contact as a person first, buyer second, strengthens the friendship bond between seller and buyer.

Here's a casual conversational exercise for you to practice before making cold calls. The next time you enter a friend's house, look around until something new or unusual catches your eye. Then ask questions that will pry loose a story or two. For example, if you ask questions that begin with the word *when*, you will be amazed at the golden tidbits your friend will cough out.

Examples:

Alice, when did you get that beautiful plant? (Alice takes off on the plant sale she discovered last Saturday in the newspaper.)
Say, Tom, when did you find time to build the bookcase in your den?
(Tom hits you with a step-by-step account of the entire project.)

What if a prospect just doesn't have time for casual conversation? Simply skip it. Refrain from creating or fabricating front talk. It won't work unless it flows naturally from a genuine well.

Occasionally meeting a prospect for the first time puts the nervous system on guard. This normal reaction is your nervous system's way of girding you for action. Most experienced athletes say they are a trifle nervous before entering the arena; salespeople are no different.

Let's examine four ways to help you relax when making cold calls.

One, take two or three deep breaths. Fill your lungs with fresh air. You'll feel more energetic, more relaxed, and you'll experience a sense of well-being.

Two, form a positive image of everything around you. Let your sense receptors roam about freely. Digest your total surroundings.

Three, think in terms of forming a long-lasting relationship between you and the prospect. You'll build self-confidence in selling, and at the same time strengthen your ability to relate to people.

Four, be sure your product or service can fill a definite need. This key factor builds mutual trust between you and your prospect. You're there to help, not simply to sell. If your product or service doesn't meet a prospect's need, say so. Don't waste a prospect's time by pushing something that obviously doesn't apply.

Suppose, however, you can provide a valuable product or service and the prospect tosses a big *no* at you during the cold call. What then? Do you curl up like a pill bug and roll away? Undoubtedly, the word *no* discourages a salesperson, but a big thinker accepts the challenge of finding out why the prospect said no. A no response, for example, can mean different things from a prospective client. For instance, it might mean "definitely not" or "I'm not sure" or "I don't agree with you" or "I don't know what you're talking about" or "I don't need what you have" or "I don't think that I can afford it."

When a prospect says no you must identify and examine the reason for refusal. Here are five ways to do this:

1. Find out why without asking. Why becomes dangerous because most prospects interpret "Why?" as an argumentative question that often leads to conflict.

Express a genuine concern for your prospect's feelings. Your response might be:

YOU: Fine, Ms. Burns, I understand that now isn't the right time. If it's okay with you, I'll contact you in six or eight weeks.

If Ms. Burns has no desire to use your product or service, she's likely to tell you why rather than schedule an appointment with you.

2. When the prospect says no, stay calm and keep from showing displeasure or concern. An expressionless face coupled with a nonchalant attitude often tempts the prospect to spill forth with reasons for saying no. There's something about a silent, apathetic response to a no answer that shakes loose a feeling of guilt from within a prospect. Many prospects back up their no's with apologies that often turn the no into a definite maybe or yes! It's imperative that you stay in control during this time. If you give the slightest hint of being upset or ruffled, your prospect may build a shield that shuts down any further communication between you and the prospect.

3. Ask your prospect a pivot question. A pivot question is one that shows respect for the prospect's decision, but requires an explanation. Here is an example of a pivot question:

YOU: Ms. Cummings, obviously you have a good reason for saying that. May I ask what it is?

Don't say another word, just wait for her reply.

4. After the prospect answers the pivot question, you must determine how strong the no really is, and whether or not it's worth your time to arrange a presentation.

If you feel the prospect is going to be extremely difficult to sell, go somewhere else. Keep in mind that your product or service may not be beneficial to every prospect. Some will not be able to afford it; others will not feel a strong enough need to use it. A staunch resistance during a cold call indicates you're dealing with a prospect who, for one reason or another, simply isn't intersted in your product or service. As the prospect gives reasons for saying no, listen for clues that might open the door for further negotiations.

5. Remain silent. Let the prospect talk. The more the prospect talks, the weaker the no becomes. Often a prospect gets so wound up in an explanation that he inadvertently talks himself into

an appointment. If, however, you have a strong point to make, then by all means make it. But remember to let your prospect finish his explanation first. A series of interruptions leads to frustration and places your prospect on the defensive.

A good rule to remember is: Be patient, stay calm, listen hard, and have a genuine concern for your prospect's needs. Your sincerity and thoughtfulness will lead to a higher ratio of cold calls to scheduled sales presentations.

3. Maintain flexibility at all times

Nature has provided the Willow Beauty moth with the ability to blend its wing pattern to match the color of bark. The moth can also position its body to eliminate shadows from its wings. Now that's adaptability. A wise salesperson, like the Beauty moth, learns early to be flexible and avoid serious problems.

Maintaining flexibility in your cold calling approach means being able to adjust to any situation without causing undue stress on you or your prospect. In many instances, cold calling taxes your ability to deal with apathetic prospects.

Prospects aren't born with apathetic genes nestled in their chromosomes. What usually turns them off are the salespeople who hit them between the eyes with a rigid cold calling presentation, one that smacks of memorized passages from a company brochure. Hence, a salesperson risks losing future customers. A stiff, mechanical approach spawns apathetic responses like these:

"Hold it. Save your breath. I'm not interested."
"Will this take long? I'm really busy, you know."
"Just leave your card. I'll try to call you later."

You can't survive in today's competitive market without being flexible in your cold-calling approach. Flexibility requires endurance, persistence, and a keen sense of timing. So in order to develop flexibility, you must:

1. Prepare yourself for the worst possible situation. Don't expect a warm greeting and a slap on the back when you meet a prospect, especially if it's a first-time meeting. You must prepare yourself for the prospect who doesn't share your enthusiasm and

cuts your cold call short with a sharp "no!" If you counter with a stilted memorized presentation, your cold calling attempt will fall flat.

Often a no response is simply a spontaneous remark, not a personal attack on you. Also, some people believe a yes response is like waving a white flag. To them, yes signifies weakness. By showing understanding instead of disdain you come through as a friend, not an adversary.

A good way to do this is by "going negative" with a prospect; that is, listen quietly as the prospect sounds off. Show understanding for your prospect's dilemma by acquiescing at the right time. Empathizing with a prospect makes good sense. After all, it's difficult to dislike someone who agrees with you.

2. Ask pertinent questions that will eventually swing the conversation toward the virtues of your product. For example, if you are attempting to interest a sporting goods store owner (we'll call him Mr. Charles) in newspaper advertising, you might ask the following questions:

"Mr. Charles, what are your future plans for expanding your store?"
"Mr. Charles, do you feel your competitors have an advantage over you?"
"Mr. Charles, what do you feel is your biggest problem as a store owner?"

By asking relevant questions you get the prospect to think about business, not which exit to send you through. As the prospect hammers away on future business ideas, your chances of success improve because it's tough to talk about future business expansion without a sound advertising plan. And that's exactly why you're there, right?

It takes an intelligent observer to ask questions that encourage a prospect to reveal his or her needs. Naturally this must transpire in a pressure-free environment.

3. Identify and expand on your prospect's needs. Then schedule a sales presentation to show your prospect how your product or service will meet these needs.

Take your time and let your prospect evaluate the situation. Don't be overanxious to make an appointment and run. The more information that you accumulate during a cold call, the better your chances will be of making a sale during the actual presentation.

4. If you feel good about a prospect, use a nonchalant persistence in getting the appointment. This, above all, requires considerable self-control. Have enough faith in your product or service and in your prospect's ability to make the right decision. Conclude your business in an easy, relaxed manner.

Does flexibility provide some of the magic for doubling or tripling your income? Yes, it does. For example, Steve R., advertising salesman, earned $16,000 his first year. He nearly quit selling because, as he put it, merchants were "drowning in an ocean of salespeople."

In 1979, Steve attended my seminar held in San Francisco entitled "Flexibility: The Key to Successful Cold Calling." This session featured a five-step approach to flexibility in action by providing a series of role-playing situations.

Last year I received a phone call from Steve. He mentioned that he had attended the San Francisco seminar and told me how the flexibility plan had payed off for him. Here, in part, is what Steve told me:

> My main problem was putting your flexibility ideas into practice. At first, I found it extremely difficult to change an established cold-calling routine. Little by little, however, I began to feel more comfortable with your plan, which, to say the least, is quite unconventional.
>
> Your plan scores a Triple A rating, Jon. Last year I earned nearly $30,000, and if things continue to go well for me, I'll make close to $40,000 this year.

The following tips will help you build a flexible cold calling presentation:

- Begin with small talk. Put you and your prospect at ease. *Note:* If your prospect keeps glancing at his watch, you're probably spending too much time talking about the weather or grandma's homemade cookies.
- Be yourself. Match your cold call presentation to fit your personality.

- Speak in a relaxed, conversational tone. Let the words flow naturally.

- Refrain from giving a prospect the cost of your product or service during a cold call. Giving a price before the prospect sees a presentation is like fishing with a barbless hook— you'll lose nine out of ten fish.

Suppose a prospect asks for a price. What then? It really depends on what product or service you are selling. Here's one answer you might give:

Ms. TURNER: How much will your service cost me?

YOU: Ms. Turner, there are many variables to consider. I can, however, give you a price as soon as I have a chance to examine your specific needs.

Ms. TURNER: How long will that take?

YOU: It only takes about fifteen minutes. In fact, I'd do it for you right now, but I'm already late for an appointment. Would this Thursday at 9:45 a.m. or Friday at 2:15 p.m. be best for you?

- Believe in your product and prospect. If you do, here's a promise: The good days will outnumber the bad, again and again.

- Be tactful. Keep several cold calling action plans on file in your memory bank. If Plan One sputters, switch to Plan Two or Plan Three. In other words, be ready to match the right cold calling approach with the present situation.

4. Getting the prospect to feel comfortable

As stated previously, a low-key approach takes the tension out of cold calling and puts both salesperson and prospect at ease. However, your ability to quickly size up a situation and adjust accordingly determines how a prospect will react to you.

The following example shows what can happen to you if you fail to empathize with a prospect.

YOU: Good morning, nice day isn't it?

PROSPECT: Not so far. What can I do for you? (*Tip:* Something's wrong, go easy.)

YOU: (pointing to a stuffed deer head on the wall) Say, did you shoot it?

PROSPECT: (growing impatient) No, it has been here since I bought the store. What do you need? (*Tip:* Short, curt answers. Say "No, just looking." Then leave. Plan to return later.)

YOU: Ah, yeah. My name is Don Atwood. The reason I stopped by was because ... (*Tip:* You stayed one statement too long. In short, your timing and good sense were both off.)

Obviously, a casual approach or any other approach for that matter won't succeed as long as the prospect remains unreceptive. Whenever a prospect appears troubled or in a sour mood, it's best to leave and come back at a later, more congenial time.

A good way to get a prospect to feel comfortable is by using a lighthearted, jovial approach. Show that you truly like what you are doing and enjoy working with people who can benefit from your product or service.

Here are two suggestions for creating a comfortable atmosphere:

1. Listen hard. Take mental notes on what the prospect says. Then mentally rank these comments according to the importance the prospect places on them.

For example:

Prospect's Comments	Important	Unimportant
I'm a staunch Republican.	Yes	
The new Cadillac looks silly.		Yes
My business has been slipping lately.	Yes	
Halibut's okay, but I'm not too crazy about salmon.		Yes

If applicable, lend support to important comments in a sincere way. If you disagree with any of the comments, remain silent, and when the opportunity occurs, change the subject.

To stress a point, several years ago a friend of mine lost a potential sale because he didn't listen carefully to what the prospect said. During the cold call, the prospect stated that times were rough because there was "too much damned government spending." My friend countered with, "Naw, you can't blame the government. It's doing the best it can."

2. Say what you have to say. Then leave. Be conservative with a prospect's time. Make each minute count by coming quickly to the point and letting the prospect know your intentions. Nothing distracts or annoys a prospect more than a salesperson who sneaks about like a neighborhood thief.

5. Getting the prospect to talk

A prospect must talk. Clearly, that's the most effective way you'll learn anything about a prospect's interests, immediate concerns, future expectations, and so on.

How does a big thinker extract precious tidbits of information during a cold call? Here are two ways:

1. Ask interesting questions. You can tell almost immediately if a question has merit by the emotional response that accompanies the answer. Does the prospect frown or laugh out loud? Does the prospect smirk or smile? Does the prospect look at you or turn away? Watch closely. Stick with those questions that produce a favorable reaction.

2. Respond to a prospect in an interesting manner. What are some interesting human characteristics? A psychologist surveyed more than 2,000 people and asked them, "What traits interest you the most in others?" She came up with a list of the ten most popular reported traits. They are as follows: attractive physical appearance, pleasing disposition, sincerity and understanding, positive attitude, high ambition, sense of humor, common interests and goals, compassion, thoughtfulness, and intelligence.

As a big-thinking salesperson, one of your prime concerns should be to present yourself in a bright, lively fashion every time you make a cold call. If you do, your ratio of cold calls to scheduled sales presentations will show steady improvement.

6. Getting the prospect to like you

Before you can get a prospect to like you, you must like the prospect. Again, your reactions during a cold call set the tone for success or failure.

With few exceptions, a prospect will respond positively toward you if you create a happy, relaxed atmosphere that encourages conversation.

There are three techniques that favor the big-thinking salesperson when dealing with prospects during cold calls. They are:

- Treat the prospect as the most important person in the world.
- Let music flow from your presentation by feeling excited about how your product or service will benefit the prospect. Let the tone of your voice carry the message.
- Come off as being likeable.

Finally, an interesting event happens when you allow a prospect to speak: The more the prospect talks and the harder you listen, the better conversationalist the prospect will think you are.

7. Getting the prospect to want to see your product or service

If you can show a prospect how your product or service can save money, time, improve production, or simply make life easier, then you'll have little trouble scheduling a sales presentation. In fact, you might make an on-the-spot presentation. Here's a possibility:

PROSPECT: If I could get away more often, I'd spend more time fishing.

SALESPERSON: Well Bill, that's the reason I wanted to see you today. Our new machine can save you up to 32 hours a month. Now that would give you extra time to fish.

PROSPECT: It sure would.

SALESPERSON: If you have a moment, Bill, I'll show you now.

PROSPECT: Hey, let's do it!

A prospect will be more receptive to schedule a sales presentation with you if you do these things:

- Act with enthusiasm
- Know your product or service; firmly believe in what you are doing
- Center your cold call approach on the prospect's immediate concerns
- Go with the flow, stay flexible, and be ready to shift directions if necessary
- Act professional at all times

8. Establishing a power position during conversation

We've stressed how questioning becomes a powerful tool in the hands of a big-thinking salesperson. You've seen how asking intelligent, interesting questions encourages a prospect to open up and talk to you. Also, it becomes apparent that through conversation you learn exactly what a prospect needs and can afford. By asking these timely questions you gain full control of the cold call and the prospect's confidence.

To retain the power position of the conversation, you must build your cold call presentation around those events that have a direct bearing on your prospect. How can you do this?

First, do a little homework. Find out how your prospect maintains his business. Sleuth around. Ask the janitor, the secretary—anyone connected with the business. You can pick up a carload of tips that will really help you during your cold call confrontation.

Second, have your questions ready in advance. Fumbling around for things to ask leads to confusion and marks you as an amateur.

Third, ask questions that lead directly into your cold call. Combine timing with tact. Remember, you gain control of a conversation by listening first, asking questions second.

Last point: Your attitude during conversation often determines how effective your cold call will be. You must convince the prospect that your product or service will, in some way, benefit his business.

A big thinker does this by acting in a calm, relaxed manner. A "hungry for a sale" approach scares prospects away.

These are three simple closes a master cold caller might try:

> "Carl, let me stop by tomorrow and show you our new service. It only takes 25 minutes, okay?"
> "Mr. Clark, I'd like you to look at our new product. If you like what you see, we'll get together and set something up. If not, no problem. Okay?"
> "Ms. Lange, let me stop by and show you our new product."

A smooth cold call close sounds good to you and your prospect. A "nonsale" approach minimizes stress and keeps a prospect from stumbling about searching for excuses not to see you again. So stick with the cold call close that consistently brings you positive results. You're sure to reach your big-thinking objectives sooner.

A BIG THINKER'S LIST OF COLD CALLING DO'S

Let's review the strong points of cold calling by listing them under cold calling do's.

COLD CALLING DO'S

1. Think, speak, and present yourself in a positive way. Do the same for your product or service.

2. Be enthusiastic. Know what you are about and believe in what you are doing.

3. Seek out qualified prospects. Concentrate on meeting their needs and interests.

4. Ask questions that show intelligence and express your concern for the prospect's welfare.

5. Be an active listener.

6. Present yourself as being friendly.

7. Shoot for a high percentage of scheduled sales presentations.

8. Strive for improvement by establishing a workable cold call plan of action.

9. Record your daily or weekly cold call results by graphing the information. Then use the results to help you increase your ratio of cold calls to scheduled sales presentations.

10. Speak in a relaxed, casual manner. Let your voice carry a musical message. Treat a prospect as a friend, and someone you'd like to work with on a long-term basis.

11. Keep the front talk casual, interesting, and centered on the prospect's desires and concerns.

12. Allow the prospect to do most of the talking.

13. Keep your presentation flexible. Be ready to adjust your presentation without causing undue stress on yourself or your prospect.

14. Enjoy your work and allow others to feel good about your presence.

15. Respect a prospect's time. Keep your visit short and to the point.

POINTS TO REMEMBER

For some salespeople, just the thought of making cold calls sends shivers down their spines. But as a big-thinking, mature salesperson, you know it takes self-confidence, common sense, and legwork to come up with qualified leads. You realize the value of doing your best at every facet of selling.

You are also aware of how a strong, positive attitude goes hand-in-hand with a burning desire to succeed. How successful you become hinges on several factors. Some of these are: 1) a belief in your product, prospect, and yourself; 2) your ability to adapt to new situations; 3) your ability to build a strong customer relationship; 4) your determination to improve your listening skills; 5) your ability to recognize the needs of prospects; and 6) your ability to control a conversation and extract information valuable to both you and your prospect.

CHAPTER FOUR

BUILDING AND MAINTAINING A BIG THINKER'S SELLING PACKAGE

n this chapter you'll receive big-thinking tips and suggestions on how to prepare yourself in a positive way for giving outstanding sales presentations.

You'll learn how to tell in advance if your prospect wants to hear your presentation or intends to buy your product or service.

You'll see how tag lining and tracking, techniques covered in earlier chapters, can help you strengthen your total selling package.

You'll discover how your daily scorecard and weekly tally card serve as excellent predictors for future selling success.

Last, you'll see how your selling efforts fit into the Master Selling Plan, which is designed to double or triple your earnings.

PREPARING YOURSELF FOR THE SALES PRESENTATION

Nobody knows you as well as you do, and nobody can control the flow of conversation or the direction your sales presentation will go better than you. Therefore, in this section, we'll explore the following areas:

1. The magic of getting to know yourself
2. What you should know about your product or service
3. Do you need to change your selling approach? (a self-test)
4. Four ways to develop a winning sales personality

1. The magic of getting to know yourself

Are you truly a big-thinking salesperson with a sincere desire to double or triple your earnings? You can find out by asking yourself these questions:

- Do I have a written plan of action that includes realistic goals?
- Am I attaining these realistic goals within a reasonable length of time?
- Does the plan of action fit my Master Selling Plan?
- Am I preparing myself adequately for meeting the daily challenge of selling?
- *How* am I preparing myself adequately for meeting the daily challenge of selling?
- What special problems am I facing as a salesperson?
- What steps am I taking to find solutions to these problems?

The ideal answers, of course, are yes, yes, yes, yes, by ... (list several ways), none or short list, and none or short list.

The magic of reaching your big-thinking objective centers on your willingness to honestly evaluate yourself on a daily basis. By continually asking yourself these seven questions, you know what you're about at all times.

2. What you should know about your product or service

Without question, you must have sufficient information about your product or service to get a fast, positive start. Even as a big thinker you might say or do things that return to haunt you, but learning from these mistakes is how you'll develop sales maturity.

Don't be embarrassed to say "I don't know" when a prospect asks a difficult question. Few salespeople know everything about their product or service. An honest answer tells the prospect that you really do care. As an example, a prospect says, "Hey, will this product remove the scales from my tuna boat?" Your answer might be, "I'm not sure. Try it and see. If it works, great. If not, return it and get a refund."

Keep in mind that your product or service may not be for everybody since individual needs vary considerably. Even an experienced salesperson slips on occasion and tries to sell an item that doesn't excite a prospect.

In some instances the reputation of a product or service, not the salesperson, does the selling. As an example, when I was going to college and working part-time in an upholstery shop, I remember a shoe salesman who came around two or three times a year. He was a plump, balding gentleman with a soft voice. He would walk through the shop announcing, "Shoes, shoes. Need some shoes?" Ironically, he did very well. In fact, he was a top salesperson for his company. Was it his vibrant personality, his dynamic power over prospects? No, he sold a popular brand of shoes known for long-lasting quality.

Know the features of your product or service well enough to anticipate the questions your prospect might ask. A good way to do this is by thinking like a prospect. In other words, if you were a prospect listening to the sales presentation, what questions are you likely to ask? Some of these may include the following:

1. How will this product or service help me personally?
2. What are the advantages of buying this product or service?
3. Do I really need this product or service *now*?
4. What must I consider before purchasing this product or service?
5. Can I buy this product or service without creating a financial burden for myself?
6. Is there a product or service of equal quality on the market for the same price?
7. What evidence do I have that this product or service will work for me?

Last point: Avoid using the reputation of your product or service as a replacement for excellent salesmanship; 99 percent of the time it won't work. Remember, if you think as a prospect, you'll be more apt to recognize actual needs.

3. Do you need to change your selling approach? (A self-test)

You saw in Chapter 3 how flexibility in cold calling often spells the difference between success and failure. The same basic principle holds true for giving sales presentations: If you want to grow and make big money in selling, you must constantly seek ways to strengthen your selling approach. The problem is how.

You can do this by checking your selling results on a daily basis. Then ask yourself: Am I happy with my current income? Am I keeping pace with my Master Selling Plan? If your answer to both questions is no, then find a sheet of paper, number one through nine, and read each of the following questions or statements carefully. Answer by writing T for true, F for false, and NS for not sure.

1. Do you feel that it's your responsibility to identify the true needs of a prospect?

2. Should you create a need when your prospect seems puzzled or confused?

3. You discover that your prospect really can't use your product or service. Should you create a need so as not to lose a potential customer?

4. Encourage a prospect to use pure reason rather than emotion when evaluating the quality of your product or service.

5. Ask your prospect questions that encourage yes answers. This keeps your prospect thinking positively.

6. It's really not necessary to anticipate the reasons your prospect may not want to buy your product or service.

7. Be prepared ahead of time by arming yourself with standard counterpoints when a prospect rejects your product or service.

8. In many instances a prospect buys the salesperson first, the product or service second.

9. The reputation of your product or service should be enough to tell a prospect whether or not to buy.

Here's how a big thinker would answer: 1. yes; 2. no; 3. no; 4. no; 5. yes; 6. no; 7. no; 8. yes; 9. no.

These answers alone are not sufficient to suggest changing your selling approach. You need to know why these are big-thinking responses and how a big thinker can apply these income-producing techniques. A breakdown of these techniques is shown in Figure 4-1.

In this chapter we'll examine productive ways in which a big thinker can increase his or her selling ratio of presentations to sales.

4. Four ways to develop a winning sales personality

By now you know yourself well and how to present your product or service in a professional manner. You also have your sights set on becoming a big-thinking salesperson. Now let's examine four ways to develop a winning sales personality.

First, you become a big-thinking winner when you successfully reach your goals in a reasonable length of time. Your first step, of course, is to write down your goals and refer to them frequently. These affirmations become rules to live by, constant reminders to keep pushing forward.

A friend of mine, Julie Simmons, sells real estate in Southern California. She earned over $65,000 last year. Her profit margin over the last two years jumped tremendously. Her secret? She carries written affirmations with her at all times. More specifically, she keeps several cards in her purse with positive messages written on them. She reads these cards over many times during the day.

She told me, for example, that when she takes her coffee break, she reaches for her cards and reads each one. She says this routine serves to keep her mind occupied with positive thoughts. Three of her cards read as follows:

> Today is all mine. A big sale
>   awaits me.
> I will keep reaching. I'm well
>   on my way to the top.
> Somebody needs me today. I'll
>   be ready to help out.

Reading affirmations regularly helps you stay on target and allows you to keep pace with your Master Selling Plan. Let's say, for instance, that you elect to follow the Master Selling Plan outlined in Chapter 1. Your major goal is to earn $68,000 in the next two years. Looking back, you see that Section B, Goal Statements 2 and 3, read as follows:

Figure 4-1

Answer		This is a *big thinking* response because....	A *big thinker* can apply this information in the following manner:
1	Yes	You know better than anyone what your product or service can and can't do.	Once you discover a prospect's needs (through listening and asking questions), you can match the product or service to fit the need.
2	No	There must be an actual need, not one created out of passion.	Take your time. Work slowly and carefully until your prospect understands how your product or service can benefit him.
3	No	Forcing a product or service that cannot benefit a prospect stirs up hard feelings.	Ask prospect for referrals—someone else who might be able to use your product or service.
4	No	Pure reason alone leaves the prospect with a cold, shallow impression of your product or service.	Reasoning implies a thinking, mechanical behavior. An emotional appeal asks the prospect to *feel* satisfied before buying.
5	Yes	A positive atmosphere produces positive selling results.	A steady flow of yes responses makes the prospect more receptive to buying your product or service.
6	No	Anticipation of a prospect's response puts you one step ahead.	Through anticipation, you prepare yourself to make necessary adjustments in your selling approach.
7	No	You should never use standard counterpoints because every selling situation is unique.	Treat every prospect and selling situation as a unique experience. Be ready to change or shift directions when necessary.
8	Yes	You know the importance of making a favorable first impression.	Approach each prospect with self-confidence, enthusiasm, and high hopes of satisfying individual needs.
9	No	An excellent reputation doesn't guarantee that the prospect's needs will be met.	Use a strong reputation to publicize quality, but make sure the product or service can actually help your prospect.

2. Increase concentration and money-making aspect of selling.

3. Keep a big-thinking, positive outlook on selling.

Your written affirmations for each goal statement might appear like this:

2. Increase concentration and money-making aspect of selling. *Affirmations*:

I will read and study what others are
   doing to find success.
I will listen and keep an open mind to
   what others are saying.
I will ask intelligent questions and look
   for better ways to sell myself and my
   product or service.

3. Keep a big-thinking, positive outlook on selling. *Affirmations*:

Sell. Sell today. Do it now!
Each sale brings me one step closer
   to my major objective.
I will think, plan, sell, and be big.

Again, keep your affirmations centered on attainable goals and you'll reach your big-thinking objective within your designated time limit.

The second way to develop a winning sales personality is to keep your adrenalin flowing and spirits high by surrounding yourself with people who display winning attitudes. Some people talk big but produce little. Stay away from these individuals; they tend to blame others for their failures.

How can you spot winners in the selling profession? They are those who:

- Know where they are going and what it takes to get there.

- Set realistic goals and take active steps to reach them.

- Think, speak, and act in a positive way.

- Continue to seek better ways to sell their product or service.

- Deal with daily stress in a calm, rational manner.
- Stay in total control of the selling scene at all times.
- Consider prospects to be the most important people in the world.
- Keep up to date on current events, including modern selling techniques.
- Monitor their selling progress on a daily, weekly, and monthly basis.

Third, scout around for those books and magazine articles that stress the importance of developing and maintaining a positive mental attitude. They carry an upbeat, challenging message for big thinkers to live by: Hard work yields satisfying rewards.

Julie Simmons reads a lot. She extracts bits of information that parallel her thinking regarding selling philosophy. Julie designs affirmations around the thoughts gleaned from her reading.

Here's the bottom line: Nobody can stop you from reaching your major goal if you make a personal commitment to do these things:

1. Read and study the advice of successful people you admire.
2. Extract the information that matches your selling style and beliefs.
3. Include the information in a practical plan that you can put into immediate use.
4. Continue to search for new ideas that will strengthen your selling program.
5. Share positive results with others. This opens the door for widespread communication.

Fourth, combine the foregoing steps and include them in your big-thinking selling package. The magical ingredient necessary to pull all of this together is *consistency*. Do these things every day, 365 days a year. Be consistent and watch your selling performance come alive.

In review, mix with winning salespeople and continually seek ways to improve. Follow the advice of those who choose to share their good fortune.

Finally, here are three suggestions for setting up affirmations: One, keep them short and to the point; two, make them challenging and commensurate with your major objective; three, inject them with an emotional, positive flavor.

Your Winning Sales Personality Cycle develops in the manner shown in Figure 4-2.

FIGURE 4-2

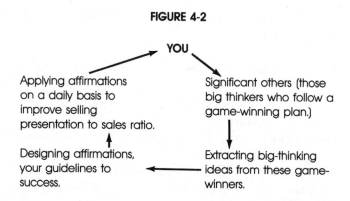

PREPARING YOUR PROSPECT FOR THE SALES PRESENTATION

After you prepare yourself for the sales presentation, your next step is to ready the prospect for the sales presentation. In this section, then, we'll examine these five areas:

1. How to find out if your prospect is in a listening mood
2. Getting and holding your prospect's attention
3. Dealing effectively with your prospect's emotions
4. Tailoring your sales presentation to a prospect's need
5. How to tell if your prospect is ready to buy

1. How to find out if your prospect is in a listening mood

Your opening question often tells you immediately how receptive your prospect will be. If a "How are you doing today?" salutation brings a "Terrible so far" response, go easy. That's a tip things could be better. Therefore, without a doubt, the best way to find out is by simply asking.

A big thinker, under these conditions, steps softly and does nothing to intimidate the prospect. Other obvious clues that signal trouble ahead are tone of voice, facial expressions, eye contact (lack of), attention span, and the manner in which a prospect answers your questions.

Some prospects are real pros at hiding their moods or true feelings. They wait until you're well into your sales presentation before cutting you off. This, of course, dampens your selling spirit and slows down your momentum. Happily, in many cases, reluctant prospects waste little time revealing how they feel.

As a big-thinking salesperson, you want only those prospects who care to listen. How can you tell if your prospect shares your enthusiasm or wishes to hear what you have to say? Here are seven telltale signs of a good listener:

1. A prospect will definitely listen and refrain from asking unrelated questions to throw you off the track.

2. A prospect will look and act interested by making eye contact, acquiescing to show agreement, asking intelligent questions.

3. A prospect will empathize with you and try to understand your point of view.

4. A prospect will allow you to speak and limit the number of distractions.

5. A prospect will provide a quiet, peaceful environment for you to give your sales presentation.

6. A prospect will remain calm and not appear too pressed or in a hurry to go somewhere.

7. A prospect will treat you with respect and courtesy.

If your prospect demonstrates these behaviors, you can be sure your prospect cares.

2. Getting and holding your prospect's attention

Let's first consider how to *get* your prospect's attention. Some people shout, whistle, or scream to draw attention. Big-thinking salespeople, however, handle prospects in a more congenial way.

Undoubtedly you have special techniques that work well for you. Here are six attention getters that bring positive selling results:

One, create interest by carrying on a casual, pressure-free conversation with your prospect. Speak softly and clearly. Use well-chosen words in a convincing manner.

Two, know ahead of time what questions you intend to ask. For example,

> "Ms. Turner, what is your most pressing need at the moment?"
> "In what way can I be of help to you, Mr. Stark?"
> "Give me ten minutes, Ms. Collins, to show you a plan that will save you $10,000 this year, okay?"

This is really simple to do. You know your product or service and how it can possibly benefit your prospect, so your questions will naturally center on your prospect's need. Also, by planning ahead you won't have to juggle facts and ideas while speaking; you can relax enough to pick up on your prospect's reactions.

Never go into a sales presentation unprepared to ask key questions. Once you rely on improvisation, your presentation begins to die, the prospect loses interest, and confusion takes over.

Three, appeal to the friendly nature of your prospect. Present yourself as being friendly and most prospects will respond to you in the same way. A low-key, nonchalant selling approach puts the prospect at ease and provides a permissive environment for the free exchange of ideas.

Four, create a series of questions that will get the prospect to agree with you. For instance:

YOU: You certainly have a beautiful home, Mr. Clay.

MR. CLAY: Thank you.

YOU: Isn't it a crime how expensive it is to heat a home like yours?

MR. CLAY: And how. It'll cost even more next year.

YOU: My mother's home is nearly three-fourths the size of yours. She pays around $150 a month to heat hers.

MR. CLAY: I wish I could heat my place for that. It cost me over $220 last month!

YOU: That's really terrible.

MR. CLAY: Yes, but there's not much I can do about it.

YOU: Well, Mr. Clay, maybe you can. You see, our new solar heating system can reduce your heating bill by 25 percent each month.

MR. CLAY: Really?

You have Mr. Clay's attention because you're addressing a specific need. Now it becomes a matter of whether or not Mr. Clay can afford to install this new system.

Here's another example:

YOU: How many employees do you have, Ms. Kelley?

MS. KELLEY: Twelve.

YOU: That presents a sizable bookkeeping job, doesn't it?

MS. KELLEY: Yes, it does, especially in payroll.

YOU: I know what you mean. Uncle Sam seems to create new forms every year, doesn't he?

MS. KELLEY: Yes, and the red tape is giving us fits.

YOU: That's why I wanted to speak with you, Ms. Kelley. Our accounting system is designed to simplify your entire system, and at the same time reduce your accounting cost . . . here, let me show you what I mean.

A prospect will listen as long as your questions show understanding, compassion, and insight.

Five, keep your eyes on your prospect while giving the sales presentation. If you're really looking at your prospect, you'll be able to spot outward signs of his lack of interest.

Six, request a response whenever possible. If you feel your presentation has become a monologue, ask a question—and listen to the answer.

Now let's examine four ways to *hold* your prospect's attention.

One, keep your sales presentation moving at a brisk pace. Include plenty of examples and anecdotes to clarify your main points. If possible, include familiar examples—those your prospect knows something about.

Two, come to the point quickly. Front talk helps to put you and your prospect in a relaxed mood, but don't tire out your prospect before your sales presentation starts to roll.

Three, assure your prospect that your product or service will solve a problem, meet a need, or both. You can do this by demonstrating the usefulness of your product or service or by leaving samples for your prospect to test.

Four, if possible keep your sales presentation brief. Say what needs to be said and leave. A restless prospect loses concentration fast and shows signs of irritability.

3. Dealing effectively with your prospect's emotions

Some prospects evaluate a product or service through emotion rather than reason. For example, maybe the color or texture of a product becomes the force behind the purchase. Emotion has a way of entering the problem-solving process.

Big thinkers study a prospect's reactions during a sales presentation. Often an emotional prospect shows satisfaction by displaying such overt behavior as smiling or laughing, talking fast, asking questions, and behaving in an optimistic fashion. As a big-thinking salesperson you can keep your prospect at a pleasant emotional level by stressing the word *feel*. Here are three examples:

You: Ms. Casey, how do you *feel* about this product so far?

Don't you *feel*, Ms. Casey, that this program will benefit your operation?

Ms. Casey, I *feel* that this machine will enhance your entire production department and save your company thousands of dollars. How do you *feel* about it?

Never ask a prospect to evaluate a product or service by reason alone—how do you *think...* ? Think implies reasoning, which, in turn, restricts a prospect's expression of an emotional judgment.

4. Tailoring your sales presentation to a prospect's need

Once you establish a need, the next step is to show your prospect how your product or service can bring satisfying results. Big-thinking salespeople program their prospects to think "yes" during a sales presentation. You can do the same thing if you create a friendly, positive atmosphere and set up a series of statements or questions that will encourage a prospect to agree with you.

Let's say, for example, that you are selling copy machines and you're talking with a prospect who owns a real estate agency. Here's the conversation:

> YOU: Mr. Willis, most agency owners I've talked with aren't sure if this machine would pay for itself. How do you feel?
>
> MR. WILLIS: Well, in all honesty, I've been wondering the same thing.
>
> YOU: This machine will surprise you, Mr. Willis. Since it produces copies in seconds, your salespeople will be spending less time in the office and more time in the field, or on the phone.
>
> MR. WILLIS: Yes, time alone would be a big savings.
>
> YOU: This machine will also save you more than two cents per copy. I can show you how your agency can save over $70 each month. I feel that's a substantial savings, don't you Mr. Willis?
>
> MR. WILLIS: I sure do.

By getting a prospect to think "yes," he or she will definitely examine the advantages of using your product or service. Once a prospect's thoughts flow in a buying direction, your sales presentation takes off like a sprinter in a 100-yard dash.

A series of statements or questions that encourage a prospect to think "yes" will do these things:

1. Set the stage for affirmative action.
2. Show a prospect that you recognize and address your presentation to a definite need.
3. Anticipate the thoughts and concerns of a prospect.
4. Point up the features of your product or service that will please your prospect.
5. Boost a prospect's confidence in your selling ability.
6. Build your self-confidence as a big-thinking salesperson.

5. How to tell if your prospect is ready to buy

You can usually tell if a prospect intends to buy before and during your sales presentation. The following five-point observation for each selling phase provides enough clues to give you an indication of how successful you will be.

These are only predictors based on past experience. A big thinker sees them as a formidable challenge, a chance to test one's selling ability.

BEFORE SALES PRESENTATION

A. Good chance to sell
   1. Prospect friendly; talkative
   2. Prospect makes good eye contact; listens attentively
   3. Prospect asks questions, listens to answers
   4. Prospect makes you feel comfortable
   5. Prospect reveals immediate needs
B. Fair chance to sell
   1. Prospect reserved, doesn't say much
   2. Prospect looks away, pays half attention
   3. Prospect asks only one or two simple questions
   4. Prospect cordial, but not especially friendly
   5. Prospect doesn't pinpoint specific needs
C. Poor chance to sell
   1. Prospect quiet; apprehensive
   2. Prospect showing no interest at all
   3. Prospect doesn't ask any questions
   4. Prospect inconsiderate, almost rude
   5. Prospect doesn't reveal needs

DURING SALES PRESENTATION

A. Good chance to sell
   1. Prospect excited about product or service
   2. Prospect listens to entire sales presentation
   3. Prospect able to purchase product or service
   4. Prospect sees how product or service will enhance business
   5. Prospect carefully examines every aspect of sales presentation
B. Fair chance to sell
   1. Prospect concerned, but not too anxious
   2. Prospect interrupts sales presentation by answering phone, talking to someone else, and so on

3. Prospect's ability to purchase product or service is questionable
4. Prospect not sure how product or service will enhance business
5. Prospect not concerned with details of sales presentation

C. Poor chance to sell
1. Prospect displays a lackadaisical attitude
2. Prospect has to leave to go somewhere
3. Prospect unable to purchase product or service at present time
4. Prospect doesn't see any way product or service will enhance business
5. Prospect not impressed with any part of the sales presentation

A prospect seldom falls neatly into a good, fair, or poor category. Some may take on a combination of features from each category. As an example, a prospect may be friendly, but not interested in buying your product or service.

Remember, even a prospect who falls into the poor chance column may change his mind and buy. Again, as a big thinker you must accept the challenge of persuading a hard-to-sell prospect to buy your product or service.

A BIG THINKER'S APPROACH TO ANALYZING A SALES PRESENTATION

In this section we'll investigate seven ways to examine the productivity of your sales presentation. They are:

1. The sales presentation itself
2. How to dissect and examine your sales presentation
3. How tag-lining magic boosts your earnings
4. Checking your daily scorecard
5. Checking your weekly tally cards
6. Finding out if you're on track
7. How to put your Master Selling Plan into action

1. The sales presentation itself

The sales presentation provides the sting behind the driving force of your selling program. It, like an automobile engine, must function properly to keep everything in step. There are times, of course, when a sales presentation stalls and loses power. Here's when it's imperative for you to slow down and take a critical look at your sales presentation and how you are handling it. You must ask yourself these questions:

1. Is my prospect qualified to buy this product or service?
2. Am I putting forth a 110 percent effort behind every presentation?
3. Am I stressing the high points of my product or service?
4. Does my prospect really need this product or service?
5. Am I following a tangible plan of attack?
6. Am I sticking to a specific game plan?
7. Have I put my game plan in writing?
8. Am I monitoring my selling progress on a consistent basis?

A no response to any of these questions may indicate trouble ahead and prevent you from reaching your big-thinking objective.

As an example, two years ago Bill Alexander told me during lunch one day that he was seriously considering leaving the selling profession. He sold newspaper advertising to local merchants in a medium-sized city. Two things bothered Bill: One, his easygoing manner made it too easy for a prospect to say no; two, he lacked confidence when it came to close a sale. (His answer to Question 2 would undoubtedly be no.)

Bill decided to take action. He enrolled in an assertive selling program and changed from a sensitive, apologetic individual to a big-thinking, authoritative person. During this transformation period Bill strengthened his sales presentation by adding fire to some of the lifeless statements.

In his original sales presentation, for instance, Bill would ask: "When would be the best time to run the ad, in Wednesday's or Friday's newspaper?" A prospect would often reply, "I'm not sure.

Let me give it some thought. I'll get back to you next week." Now Bill doesn't ask. Instead he says, "Wednesday's is the most widely read newspaper. So I'll reserve a three-quarter page ad for next Wednesday."

Bill mentioned that if a prospect balked, he would continue with ... "Well, look, we could go a half page, but the larger ad is far more effective. A three-quarter page ad dominates the whole page and gives you full-page advantage for less money."

Bill's closing ratio has increased steadily since he restructured his sales presentation and transformed himself into a self-confident, big-thinking salesperson. His earnings have more than doubled in the last two years.

Final point: Your selling personality and sales presentation must be compatible if you intend to sell big. In Bill Alexander's case, he strengthened his selling character, and at the same time altered his sales presentation to match the personality change.

2. How to dissect and examine the sales presentation

A sales presentation, like your body, occasionally needs a thorough examination to make sure everything is functioning properly. This requires you to outline your sales presentation, answer certain questions, and establish a plan of action aimed toward strengthening your sales presentation. How often must you do this? There is no set time, just whenever you feel like giving your sales presentation a checkup.

In order to prepare yourself, you'll need a pen or pencil, paper, and a quiet working area. The dissection and examination process begins with a sales presentation outline, followed by key questions and an action plan for improvement.

Start by copying the following information on a sheet of paper.

SALES PRESENTATION OUTLINE

Your product or service: (Selling newspaper advertising)

A. Introduction
Briefly tell how you begin your sales presentation. List any special opening techniques you use.

(Usually with front talk. I like to establish a casual, relaxed atmosphere.)

Special Opening Techniques: (Try to center conversation on those items the prospect holds in high regard.)

B. Main Body of Sales Presentation
Briefly tell what information you include when you reach the main body of your presentation. List any special selling techniques you use.

(The advantages of advertising through the newspaper—how newspaper advertising will enhance business.)

Special Selling Techniques: (Show prospect sample ads that fit prospect's need; describe unique ways ads attract new customers.)

C. Conclusion
Briefly state how you prefer to conclude your sales presentation. List any special closing techniques you use.

(By convincing prospect that advertising through the newspaper is an economical way to increase business.)

Special Closing Techniques: (Employ Winning Sales Cycle—described in Chapter 6.)

SALES PRESENTATION QUESTIONS

A. Introduction
1. What are you doing to create enthusiasm in yourself? (Following a Master Selling Plan, monitoring selling progress, reading and studying daily affirmations, and thinking big.)
2. How are you creating enthusiasm in your prospect? (By liking what I do, constantly seeking to improve, and having faith in my product and how it can benefit others.)

3. What motivational devices do you use in your sales presentation? (Show high interest in prospect; empathize with prospect and share needs and concerns.)
4. In what way do your prospects react to these motivational devices? (In a positive manner because the sales presentation is centered on the prospect's needs and interest.)
5. Do you attract your prospect's attention immediately? How do you accomplish this? (Yes, by being friendly, energetic, and enthusiastic.)
6. How much time (average) do you spend on front talk? (Varies, from 5 to 20 minutes.)

B. Main Body of Sales Presentation
1. How do you keep your sales presentation moving at a brisk pace? (Use plenty of examples and appropriate anecdotes. Address presentation to prospect's need at all times.)
2. How do you address your sales presentation to the specific needs of your prospect? (Once the need is established, I show how product can satisfy need. Use examples and anecdotes to stress main points. Demonstrate product whenever possible.)
3. Does your sales presentation allow your prospect freedom to ask timely questions? (Yes, through low-key, nonchalant selling approach.)
4. What specific techniques do you use for keeping the flow of conversation going between you and your prospect? (Ask questions that stimulate interest and encourage prospect to discuss needs.)
5. Does your prospect fully understand the advantages of using your product or service? (Yes, these issues are brought out in the sales presentation.)

C. Conclusion
1. How did you find out if your prospect could afford your product or service? (Through observation and by asking questions related to present status of business.)
2. Are your prospects aware of your product's or service's limitations? (Yes, limitations are pointed out during the sales presentation.)
3. Do your prospects respond positively to your sales presentation? (Yes.)

In Chapter 3 you saw how to tag line your cold-calling strong points. You can follow the same procedure for examining your sales presentation. After you complete the sales presentation outline and questions, fill out an action plan for improvement. An example is shown in Figure 4-3.

3. How tag-lining magic boosts your earnings

Tag lining your strong points in the sales presentation allows you to thoroughly examine your product or service, and, to a certain degree, to gauge your success in selling your product.

Let's review the example given in Chapter 2.

Strong Points	Common Denominator
Presentation offers *quality* and *dependable* service.	
Presentation offers an *inexpensive* way to advertise.	Service will allow prospect to advertise within budget limitations and increase sales.
Presentation offers a service *comparable with competing firms.*	

You can take this example one step further and put yourself in your prospect's place by asking *how*. You need to provide clear-cut answers to such questions as: How will your newspaper ads exhibit quality? How will your newspaper ads demonstrate dependability?

Break down your strong points by listing them on paper. For instance, say *how* your product or service will do the things you state in your sales presentation. Set up your analysis in the manner shown in Figure 4-4.

The magic of tag lining comes from *showing*, not telling, your prospect. It's easy to say to a prospect, "You'll like our service. It's fast, dependable, and efficient." But as a big-thinking salesperson, you must *show* a prospect exactly *how* this is so.

Tag lining, therefore, helps you boost your earnings by constantly reminding you to show why your product or service is first-rate. It also shows the prospect that you know your product or service well and have a clear picture of what your competitors are doing. Remember, this personalized approach convinces prospects

Figure 4-3

SALES PRESENTATION ACTION PLAN FOR IMPROVEMENT

My strong points	What I need to work on	Plan of improvement	How will plan be implemented?	Evidence of success
Follow Master Selling Plan.	Keeping spirits high, day after day.	Associate with positive thinkers; read and study daily affirmations.	By simply sticking to plan of improvement.	Improved success rate in presentation to sales ratio.
Staying calm and relaxed during sales presentation.	Presenting special sales features in a clear, concise manner.	Pace self and stress key points in sales presentation.	By concentrating on this area of sales presentation.	Improved success rate in presentation to sales ratio.

The dissection and examination process serves to keep your sales presentation fresh and up to date. It also helps you to stay sharp and to reach your big-thinking objectives on schedule.

Figure 4-4

NEWSPAPER ADVERTISING	
Strong points	***How* will your product or service meet these criteria?**
Quality	By highlighting the special features of a business that attract new customers.
Dependability	By bringing out the ad on time and in the manner described.
Inexpensiveness	By comparing the cost of these ads with those on television and radio.
Competitiveness	By comparing these ads with those in other competing newspapers.

that you are a serious, hard-working person who recognizes and attends to immediate needs.

4. Checking your daily scorecard

Your daily scorecard (Chapter 2) will tell you exactly how you are selling on a day-to-day basis. Let's say your record for two weeks looks like this:

DAILY SCORECARD

Items	M	Tu	W	Th	F	Total	M	Tu	W	Th	F	Total
Presentations	4	3	5	4	7	23	3	6	4	5	8	26
Sales	1	1	2	0	2	6	1	2	2	1	2	8

Your daily presentations to sales ratio for the week of 2/5 to 2/9 and 2/12 to 2/16 is as follows:

2/5 to 2/9	2/12 to 2/16
Monday—.250	Monday—.333
Tuesday—.333	Tuesday—.333

2/5 to 2/9	2/12 to 2/16
Wednesday—.400	Wednesday—.500
Thursday— .000	Thursday—.200
Friday—.286	Friday—.250

These data suggest that your selling efficiency runs high for the first part of the week (36 percent success rate), then sales drop off (21 percent success rate). Also, you average 1.5 sales for 4.2 presentations for the first part of the week (Monday through Wednesday) and 2.5 sales for 6 presentations. A line graph of these figures is shown in Figure 4-5.

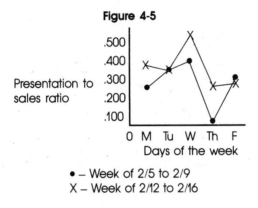

Figure 4-5

Presentation to sales ratio

Days of the week

• – Week of 2/5 to 2/9
X – Week of 2/12 to 2/16

Now you might ask yourself: Why does my selling efficiency slow down at the end of the week? Here's where an unbiased critical eye can reveal any weaknesses that creep into your sales presentation. These "negative creepers" may go unnoticed if you don't check your progress on a daily basis.

5. Checking your weekly tally cards

Your weekly tally cards (Chapter 2) include seven selling steps. Steps two through six deal exclusively with your sales presentation.

Let's see how your analysis might reveal a weakness in your sales presentation. An example is shown in Figure 4-6.

Figure 4-6

WEEKLY TALLY CARD

Week Number: <u>6</u> From: <u>2/5</u> to: <u>2/9</u>

Presenting the Proposition

23 presentations—6 sales; 17 no sales.

Problems

1. 26% success rate; 74% failure rate
2. Why 74% failure rate?
   a. Lose enthusiasm toward end of week.
   b. Schedule too many presentations at end of week. Have tendency to hurry through sales presentation.

Your strategy for corrective action might look like the example shown in Figure 4-7.

Figure 4-7

REMEDIATION

1. Sell one day at a time. Make each presentation better than the one before.
2. Concentrate on your daily affirmations. Keep them positive, fresh, and challenging.
3. Cut down on number of sales presentations. Stress quality, not quantity.

By recording and studying your weekly tally cards you pinpoint the trouble spots by analyzing each step of your sales presentation. The remediation process allows you to isolate these troublesome areas and take steps to remove them.

6. Finding out if you're on track

Chapter 1 offered four suggestions for keeping yourself on track. Must your sales presentation follow this same plan? Yes. In fact, let's see exactly how these steps can help you with your sales presentation.

1. Set a tangible plan of attack

This requires you to seek out the tips and suggestions that will provide positive ammunition for strengthening your sales presentation. An example of how your search for information develops is demonstrated in Figure 4-8.

Figure 4-8

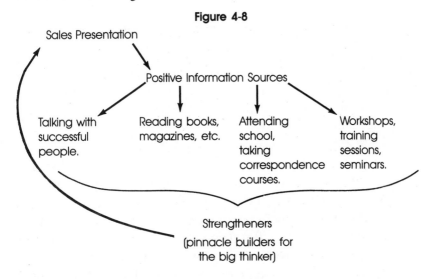

If your presentation to sales ratio slips, ask yourself: Am I turning to positive information sources to build a big-thinking selling package? Am I relying on positive information sources on a daily basis? Am I creating daily affirmations from my positive information sources?

2. Stick to your game plan

If you are satisfied with your selling results, fine. Avoid trying new methods that may throw your selling rhythm off. As long as you are meeting or exceeding your earnings at different intervals (daily, weekly, monthly), then continue to follow the same path.

3. Put your plan in writing

Check over your Master Selling Plan. Read over your goal statements and how you intend to reach these goals. Now ask yourself: Am I doing the things I said I would?

4. Closely monitor your progress

Here's the bottom line: Your weekly earnings will tell you immediately how well you've followed Steps 1, 2, and 3. Without a doubt, you'll know precisely where you stand regarding your selling progress.

7. How to put your master selling plan into action

You activate your Master Selling Plan when you do three things. They are: 1) write down your big-thinking objective; 2) list the ways in which you intend to reach your big-thinking objective; and 3) outline what you expect to accomplish as you move toward your big-thinking objective.

Here are four tips to keep in mind at all times:

1. Seek help from others. Welcome their comments, listen to their constructive criticism, and apply the suggestions that will strengthen your overall selling approach.

2. Being active doesn't necessarily mean that you are reaching your goals; therefore continue to monitor your progress daily and concentrate on staying on track.

3. Stay flexible. If you set your goals too high, adjust them to coincide with your ability, ambition, and progress.

4. Have a plan for everything you do. Look for action steps to be taken now to further your goals.

POINTS TO REMEMBER

Assessing your selling progress on a daily basis keeps you in constant touch with reality. It takes away the guesswork and lets you know exactly where you are at any given time.

You must synchronize your efforts with the needs of each prospect. In short, you must think like a prospect and examine a product or service carefully.

Be ready to change your selling approach if necessary. Do anything within reason that will allow you to obtain big-thinking results.

Mingle with people who follow a winning formula. Listen to their advice and apply the techniques that fit your selling profile.

Read and study your daily affirmations. Repeat them to yourself over and over again until they become part of your thinking process.

CHAPTER FIVE

A BIG THINKER'S APPROACH TO HANDLING OBJECTIONS

Often the toughest part of a sales presentation comes when a prospect raises an objection or purposely stalls. This action slows down your selling pace and allows confusion to take over. It also tests your patience and staying power. The manner in which you handle these objections determines to a large extent how successful you'll be as a big-thinking salesperson.

You'll see in this chapter why some prospects resist or object, how to handle these objections, and how to keep your selling machine moving in a positive direction.

The chapter will be broken down as follows:

1. Why some prospects resist more than others
2. How a big thinker breaks sales resistance
3. Big-thinking strategies for handling objections
4. Following an objection with a trial close
5. Checking your Master Selling Plan
6. Examining your self-analysis checklist
7. The magic of keeping your sales presentation moving

Let's begin with the prospect who makes selling a constant challenge for the big-thinking salesperson.

1. WHY SOME PROSPECTS RESIST MORE THAN OTHERS

It's not unusual for a prospect to raise an objection or ask a thought-provoking question during a sales presentation. Some prospects, however, seem to thrive on setting up roadblocks by asking tough questions or objections that tend to confuse and irritate the salesperson.

Why are some of your prospects more resistive to sales presentations than others? Here are eight reasons:

One, some prospects feel they must say no first. This allows them time to think about your sales presentation—that is, how the product or service will best suit their needs.

Two, some prospects aren't willing to part with their money, especially when business drops off. They want to hang on as long as possible.

Three, some prospects raise objections as a stalling tactic; that is, they use objections to delay buying your product or service at that particular time.

Four, some prospects are simply worn down by the armies of salespeople knocking on their doors.

Five, some prospects raise objections to throw you off your selling track.

Six, some prospects raise objections to show you that they are intelligent, clever, and certainly not an easy sale.

Seven, some prospects simply don't know what they want or need.

Eight, some prospects aren't interested in buying your product or service. Period.

These, of course, are just a few reasons why prospects balk and find it painful to make a decision. Other reasons for resisting are lack of confidence in your product or service, lack of confidence in the salesperson, reluctance to try a new product or service, and so on.

Now let's see how a big-thinking salesperson handles stubborn prospects.

2. HOW A BIG THINKER BREAKS SALES RESISTANCE

You probably rely on a favorite tactic for breaking sales resistance. However, there are times when even this special attempt fails to turn an objection into a sale. It's smart to keep several different ways of answering objections on hand.

Here are four big-thinking strategies that bring satisfying results:

1. Meeting an objection head-on
2. Sidestepping an objection

3. Minimizing an objection

4. Giving way to an objection

How can these strategies help you break sales resistance? Let's examine each one.

1. Meeting an objection head-on

This direct, straightforward approach requires that you be confident, assertive, and well organized. As an example, suppose you're selling sporting goods to local high schools and colleges. You've been talking with Darlene Snow, Bruster High School girls' softball coach. You're trying to sell her a pitching machine. Here's the conversation:

YOU: Coach Snow, this is the best pitching machine on the market today.

SNOW: I don't know. I have mixed feelings. I want to be sure that I purchase the best.

YOU: Believe me, our brand ranks Number One. Nothing else in its class compares with our pitching machine.

SNOW: Well, maybe, but I've heard Brand X is more accurate in delivering strikes. I'm just not sure.

YOU: Coach Snow, I can understand your feelings, but let me show you why our product is the best. (This statement demonstrates confidence and assertiveness.)

Now it's just a matter of selling your prospect on the main features of your product, including testimonials by coaches in the field or available data from those who tested the efficiency of your product.

2. Sidestepping an objection

You can sidestep an objection if you feel it really isn't a major concern of your prospect. But be careful. How you answer an objection, now matter how minor it appears to you, may be the deciding factor in winning or losing a sale.

Here's a simple technique for sidestepping an objection: When your prospect raises an objection, perhaps by asking a question or repeating something another person said, respond by asking your prospect a question. As an example, your prospect says, "According to my friend, Carl Moore, your product doesn't..." Your reply might be, "Say, thank you. You just reminded me of something. Did you know that...?"

At this point, the element of surprise has temporarily taken your prospect's mind off the objection and switched his attention to your story. This "That reminds me..." technique often wipes out your prospect's objection because your story offers a practical solution to those concerns shared by others.

3. Minimizing an objection

This technique, like sidestepping, reduces the impact of an objection. As a big-thinking salesperson you want your prospect to concentrate on the strong points of your product or service, not trivial items that tend to get in the way.

Therefore, you can keep your sales presentation moving at a steady pace by using body language to signal disapproval of objections—shrugging your shoulders, turning your head away, shaking your head from side to side, frowning, and so forth. This is an excellent way to test the strength of an objection. If your body language causes the prospect to back off or drop the objection, then you can be reasonably sure the objection had little value.

4. Giving way to an objection

Big-thinking salespeople reach their major selling goal by answering objections in a way that satisfies their prospects.

There are times when a particular objection expresses a real concern, one that cannot be answered in a realistic manner. What should you do? Simply admit, "I don't really know what to say" or "You've got me stumped. I wish I could help." After all, what can you say after a prospect hits you with, "I just haven't got the money"?

The following chart in Figure 5-1 lists four items: prospect's objection, type of objection, response to objection, and how response helps break down sales resistance. Use this chart as a guideline for setting up your own objection chart. Keep several sheets on hand and fill them out at regular intervals. By keeping track of these objections, you learn to recognize them as they develop, thus arming yourself to meet each objection squarely.

Figure 5-1

Prospect's Objection	Type of Objection	Response to Objection	How Response Helps Break Down Sales Resistance
"I don't think I should start a new service at this time."	Prospect not sure of needs or wants.	Straightforward approach. *Show why* service important *now*.	Response demonstrates confidence and assertiveness.
"Business is really bad. Come back around first of year."	Prospect not willing to part with money.	Straightforward approach. Convince prospect that service will be more expensive later.	Response emphasizes that *now* is the time to buy.
"I've heard that your product isn't that good."	Possibly stalling or objecting on basis of hearsay.	Give well-organized sales presentation backed by available facts and statistics.	Response presents updated, reliable information. Should remove doubts held by prospect.
"Hey, I'm not convinced that your product can really help me."	Prospect wants to be thoroughly convinced; prospect does not want to be an easy sale.	Be prepared to answer every question with authority. Must be confident and assertive.	Response convinces prospect that both product and sales person are first-rate.

A big-thinker's success comes from quickly recognizing the motive behind an objection. But that's only half the battle; now you must respond to each objection in an authoritative, well-organized fashion. Therefore, it becomes vital that you plan ahead for answering objections immediately.

3. BIG-THINKING STRATEGIES FOR HANDLING OBJECTIONS

In this section you'll examine eight ways to handle objections. They are as follows:

1. Let your prospect talk. Take mental notes as your prospect explains his objection. As you listen you'll be able to tell whether or not the objection lacks substance.

2. After your prospect makes his objection, simply repeat the main ideas slowly, almost as though you are surprised by what you hear. Then speak to the objection using facts to support your statements. For example:

PROSPECT: Your publication doesn't reach enough people.

YOU: You dislike our program because it doesn't reach enough people?

PROSPECT: That's right!

YOU: I don't understand. Exactly what would you consider a good publication?

PROSPECT: Any publication that gives me saturation within my market.

YOU: Do you have any in mind?

PROSPECT: Sure. The *Review* gives me good circulation.

YOU: Yes, but not saturation within the market, right?

PROSPECT: True, but excellent penetration. My cost per thousand is only 3 cents.

YOU: What is the penetration within your market?

PROSPECT: I'd say about 2,000 within one square mile of my business.

YOU: What's the cost of one insertion?

PROSPECT: About $155.

YOU: That comes out to almost 8 cents per thousand within your market.

PROSPECT: Yeah, that is expensive, isn't it?

YOU: Yes, it is.

PROSPECT: What does your publication run?

YOU: Less than one cent within your market.

PROSPECT: Maybe I should try it. What kind of circulation can you give me?

YOU: 2,600.

PROSPECT: That's very good. What'll it cost me?

YOU: $25.74 per insertion.

PROSPECT: How can you do it so cheaply?

YOU: Simple. We do not make copy changes and we concentrate our circulation within your area only.

PROSPECT: Sounds great. I'll give your service a try for the next few weeks.

This feedback method is specifically designed to stimulate a prospect's thinking process. You simply feed information to the prospect and let the prospect talk himself into buying the product or service.

3. Be believable. Answer objections in a forthright, succinct manner.

4. Welcome objections and answer them honestly. Let your prospect know that you are a responsible salesperson who takes selling seriously.

5. Confirm your response to an objection. Make sure your prospect fully understands your meaning or interpretation of an objection. For instance, after responding to an objection, ask your prospect, "Do you see what I mean?" or "Does that answer make sense?" or "Is that the answer you're looking for?"

6. After answering an objection continue with your sales presentation. A lengthy delay often invites more objections from your prospect.

7. Use the shock method to gain control of an objection. Let the element of surprise work in your favor. As an example, let's say that you're selling advertising space for a local newspaper. You walk into a grocery store and introduce yourself.

YOU: Hello, Mr. Jennings. My name is Carlene Thomas. I'm the new advertising account representative for the *Evening Blade*.

PROSPECT: I don't advertise with the *Evening Blade* after what happened last year.

YOU: Oh ... what was that?

PROSPECT: Your advertising manager, Bill Riley, promised to give me free publicity as a bonus for advertising with your paper. The only bonus he gave me was a big, fat bill. Thanks for stopping by, but I'm not interested.

YOU: Mr. Jennings, before I leave would you do something for me?

PROSPECT: Well, maybe, what is it?

YOU: Put yourself in our shoes. If you had a manager working for you who treated people like that, what would you do?

PROSPECT: Replace him immediately.

YOU: (you smile) That's exactly what we did, Mr. Jennings.

Now switch to your sales presentation and speak directly to the current needs of your prospect.

8. Answer the objection and move ahead with your sales presentation.

In summary, then, a big thinker combines several magical ingredients to respond to objections. They are as follows:

- Let your prospect do the talking while you analyze and assess the intention of the objection
- Respond to an objection with factual information
- Come directly to the point with your response
- Give a genuine response that gives comfort and support to your prospect
- Check with your prospect to make sure you are communicating and answering objection in a satisfactory manner
- Answer an objection to the best of your ability. Then continue to sell, sell, sell
- If possible, startle or surprise your prospect with key information regarding your product or service. Always have an "ace in the hole" ready at the proper time
- Keep selling

4. FOLLOWING AN OBJECTION WITH A TRIAL CLOSE

A salesman friend of mine (Mike S.) earns approximately $65,000 a year selling plastic products for a company in San Francisco. He's been with the company for the last four years. His selling secret? After answering a prospect's objection, Mike immediately follows with a trial close. Here's an example of how he does it:

MIKE: Am I right in assuming that you object to our product because of the plastic housing?

PROSPECT: Yes. I don't want anything with plastic construction.

MIKE: What you really mean, Mr. Sanders, is that you want a long-lasting product, and you don't feel plastic will do the job, right?

PROSPECT: Sure, plastic cracks too easily. Five years ago I bought a plastic shredder and had nothing but grief.

MIKE: Did the company offer to replace it?

PROSPECT: No. In fact, they acted as though they couldn't be bothered.

MIKE: Let me tell you something, Mr. Sanders. In the last two years there have been tremendous improvements with plastics. As an example, this entire housing is fully guaranteed for the life of the machine. If only one crack appears, the entire housing is replaced free of charge, labor included. Isn't that something?

PROSPECT: It sure is. They must have really perfected the product.

MIKE: They certainly did. You and I both know they wouldn't give a lifetime guarantee if the product weren't top of the line. May I set you up with a July delivery?

Mike assumes that the prospect wants to buy his product. Therefore, he hasn't anything to lose by offering to sell him his product—*now*.

Notice how Mike doesn't give Mr. Sanders much time to create more objections or excuses for not wanting to buy.

Setting up trial closes keeps your selling approach sharp. A big-thinking salespeson continually asks the magical question: "Why not give it a whirl?" Keep in mind that the more times you ask a prospect to buy, the more difficult it becomes for the prospect to refuse. Remember, an honest objection comes from a prospect who is considering your proposition. After all, if the prospect wasn't interested in buying, he wouldn't waste time objecting. So what it boils down to this: Objections come first; sales second. Objections show that your prospect is seriously considering your proposition. Therefore, as a big-thinking salesperson you should welcome objections and give intelligent responses to these objections.

5. CHECKING YOUR MASTER SELLING PLAN

A big thinker treats an objection as a challenge, not as a personal attack. Objections test the spirit and keep the mental machinery honed for action.

In Chapter 1 we mentioned how your attitude largely determines the strength of your selling package. We listed the strategy necessary for reaching the major objective of doubling or tripling your income in two years. We outlined four strategies. They are: 1) Set a tangible plan of attack; 2) stick to your game plan; 3) put your plan in writing; and 4) closely monitor your progress.

Now let's take each one and see how handling objections fits into the Master Selling Plan.

1. Set a tangible plan of attack

In your plan you might include the following:

- Ask other successful salespeople how they handle objections. Learn from their mistakes as well as their successes.

2. Stick to your game plan

- Use objections to boost your sales ratio by preparing yourself ahead of time. You can do this by anticipating objections and mentally girding yourself to answer them in a professional manner.

3. Put your plan in writing

Part B, Goal Statements of Your Master Selling Plan, lists four intentions for accomplishing your big-thinking objective. Once you

Figure 5-2

Sale   No Sale

Prospect: _____

Address: _____

_____

Date: _____

Sales Presentation

Strong Points	Weak Points

Plan for Improvement: _____

_____

_____

_____

master handling objections, each one of these intentions will reach its target.

How should you write out a plan for effectively handling objections? By filling in an objection chart at regular intervals as outlined under *How a Big Thinker Breaks Sales Resistance*.

4. Closely monitor your progress

Analyze each selling presentation by marking two columns on a piece of paper. Label the left-hand column *Strong Points* and the right-hand column *Weak Points*. Indicate *Sale* or *No Sale* at the top of the paper. Include prospect's name, address, date, and plan for improvement (See Figure 5-2). Record how well you handled objections by listing them under the appropriate column. If you list one or two under the *Weak Points* column, make sure to prescribe a plan for improvement. If your responses to objections brought favorable results, underline or star the key factors responsible for your success.

6. EXAMINING YOUR SELF-ANALYSIS CHECKLIST

Now that you have set up an objection chart as part of your monitoring process, go one step further. Fill out the *Handling Questions and Objections* section, Part F, of your self-analysis checklist described in Chapter 2.

For best results, fill out both of these forms at the same time after giving a sales presentation. Here, for your convenience, is the *Handling Questions and Objections* section:

1. Did the prospect ask many questions? _____

2. List the two most important questions your prospect asked:

   (a) _____

   (b) _____

3. Did you answer these questions with confidence? _____ Without much confidence? _____ . In a matter-of-fact fashion? _____

4. Briefly list the prospect's main objections to your presentation or product or service. _____
   _____
   _____

5. Would you consider these main objections of prime importance? _____

6. Did any objections throw off your sales presentation?
_____

7. If so, how did you handle the situation? _____
_____

8. Did you reverse any objection into a positive reason for
buying? _____

9. If so, how did you do it? _____
_____

You'll need to duplicate and run off several copies of each
form. Again, studying the results of each sales presentation allows
you to pinpoint and correct the weak spots. By recording information, you keep events fresh in your mind and mentally commit
yourself to be a big-thinking salesperson. And that's the chunk of
magic it takes to reach your major objective.

7. THE MAGIC OF KEEPING YOUR SALES PRESENTATION MOVING

You know from experience that an objection can slow down or
even stop a sales presentation cold. When this happens it's up to you
to refuel your presentation and set it flying again. What are some
effective ways to do this? Here are three:

One, keep in mind that an objection may be based on
misinterpretation. In other words, consider that your prospect may
not fully understand your words or meaning. Therefore, when a
prospect raises an objection make sure you understand the question
before giving a response. It's easy to jump the gun and listen to only
part of a question, then respond by giving an answer based on how
you *think* the prospect intended to finish the question. This
aggressive approach leads to confusion and builds antagonism
within a prospect.

Two, even if you know an objection is based on wrong
information, treat it with respect. Respond by giving accurate
information without making the prospect feel or appear foolish.

Three, present yourself as a problem solver; a person interested in making life easier for others. Do this and objections become a welcome challenge.

Last year I queried more than 200 salespeople throughout the country. I sent out a questionnaire asking these salespeople to list their selling strengths in six major areas. I received 92 replies. Question #5 asked: *Briefly describe how you handle objections from prospects during your sales presentation.* I summarized the responses and came up with a seven-point plan for handling objections without crippling your sales presentation. Here it is:

1. Listen intently to each objection. Do not interrupt.
2. Verify what you hear by repeating the objection to the prospect. Make sure you fully understand the objection.
3. Ask prospect what he thinks a satisfactory response from you should be.
4. Give an honest response based on your feelings, knowledge of product or service, and how other prospects feel.
5. Offer a solution that both you and the prospect find acceptable.
6. Remember that not all objections lend themselves to immediate or totally satisfying solutions.
7. Handle objections in a professional, but authoritative, manner. Then continue to give a first-rate sales presentation.

POINTS TO REMEMBER

You've seen how some prospects resist buying by raising objections during the sales presentation. Often many of these objections are legitimate questions regarding some aspect of your product or service. Occasionally a prospect will object just to watch you squirm; he has no intention of buying.

You've seen how to handle tough prospects by applying big-thinking strategies. As a big-thinking salesperson, you must keep track of objections and prepare mentally and physically for effective ways to handle them. You can do this by filling out an objection chart after each sales presentation. Also, you can apply the techniques suggested in Chapter 1, *Checking Your Master Selling Plan*. Finally, by filling out the *Handling Questions and Objections* section of your self-analysis checklist, you know exactly what progress you are making.

The last section lists specific ways to keep your sales presentation flowing, and offers an excellent seven-point plan for handling objections in a professional, authoritative style.

CHAPTER SIX

DEVELOPING IRONCLAD STRATEGIES FOR CLOSING SALES

You've seen how big-thinking magic can boost your earnings in three significant ways. One, by providing tips and suggestions for mastering the art of cold calling; two, by inserting success factors in strategic positions throughout your selling presentation; and three, by learning how to handle stalls and objections in a positive way.

EXAMINING CLOSING STRATEGIES FOR THE BIG THINKER

Now it's time to ready your selling machine for the big finish—closing a sale. Your success hinges on your ability and desire to employ big-thinking strategies for closing a sale. They are:

1. Developing a closer's mentality
2. Setting the stage for a strong, favorable close
3. Establishing a dynamic closing style
4. Extracting information for the big close
5. Turning objections into sales
6. Closing call backs nine times out of ten

Let's see how each of these closing techniques work to make you a topnotch, big-thinking salesperson.

1. Developing a closer's mentality

A big thinker stays alert and waits patiently for the exact moment to close a sale. This mental exercise uses a magical blend of timing and intelligence. Simply, a closer's mentality is a salesperson's awareness of opportunities to close.

How can you develop a closer's mentality? Here are four ways:

One, practice patience. Give the prospect room to make a favorable decision. Most prospects need time to think about your presentation and how your product or service will suit them best.

Two, watch every move your prospect makes. Often a slight gesture such as rubbing the chin or pulling an earlobe signals that a prospect needs further prodding before saying, "Yes, I'll take it."

Three, listen to your prospect's tone of voice. A soft, cordial tone usually emanates from a prospect who feels comfortable with you, your product or service, and the entire selling scene. Now is an excellent time to ask, "Will you take it?"

Four, if your prospect says yes, say no more. Close the sale.

2. Setting the stage for a strong, favorable close

A strong, favorable close presupposes a big-thinking philosophy of positive, hard-hitting action. You know from your own experience that positive results culminate from sound planning and logical thinking. Here, then, are solid, common-sense tips to help you prepare yourself for a powerful close:

1. Anticipate success *after* you screen your prospect. In other words, after you satisfy yourself that a prospect needs and can afford your product or service, expect to close the sale.
2. Create your own luck. Luck, for many salespeople, means being in the right place at the right time. As a big thinker, you can't afford to wait for events to occur, you must make them happen. You can do this by:

   - Molding an unbeatable attitude around self-confidence and assurance.
   - Saying things a prospect likes to hear (how your product or service will benefit the prospect personally; how your product or service will save time, effort, and energy; and so on.)
   - Catching "enthusitis" and passing along this happy spirit to your prospect. This aura of good will influences your prospect in a favorable way: to buy your product or service.
   - Think lucky. Then design your selling package to be lucky.

3. Establishing a dynamic closing cycle

Once you qualify a prospect and begin your selling presentation, you're off to a brisk start. Now you must center your efforts on keeping your prospect's thoughts and actions focused on your product or service. This will take every bit of mental muscle and experience you can muster, but the rewards will be overwhelming. Your task, at this point, is to keep the sale moving.

Occasionally a closing cycle, like a worn-out washing machine, slows down and stops. The selling beat loses its rhythm. As a result, the prospect pours out reasons for not buying. The salesperson's grip loosens, confusion takes over, and a possible sale fades away.

For example, Nancy N. worked for me as a salesperson in Carmel, California. Her yearly income averaged $15,000 for the first two years. I felt she had the ability and desire to earn two or three times that amount.

Her main problem, I discovered, came during closing. She failed to acknowledge legitimate objections voiced by prospects. She would antagonize a prospect by countering an objection with remarks like, "Oh, Mr. Stanley, don't let that bother you," or "Now don't you think you're overreacting, Mr. Bradley?" She developed a bad habit of interrupting a prospect at the wrong time while attempting, in a superficial way, to smooth out the wrinkles.

I demonstrated to Nancy (through role playing) how her caustic remarks put a prospect on the defensive. In one modeling session, I substituted her comments with, "Mr. Stanley, you have a very good point," and "I can certainly understand what you mean, Mr. Bradley, but don't you..."

Over the next eight months Nancy's selling record improved steadily. Not surprisingly, she earned nearly $23,000 the following year. By replacing cold, insensitive comments with expressions of warmth and compassion, Nancy gained self-confidence and began to blossom into a first-class salesperson.

There's a simple moral to this story: Once a prospect feels understood, he becomes more receptive to what you say—and sell.

Program your closing cycle for success every time you activate it. It works like this: You give a selling presentation to a qualified prospect. Your prospect either agrees or refuses to buy your product or service. If the prospect agrees, close the sale; end of cycle. If, however, the prospect refuses, reenter by stressing the strong points of your selling presentation. Remember, your big-thinking goal can be reached only through closing sales.

A closing cycle, like a barometer, gives a good indication of what to expect. A falling barometer suggests stormy weather ahead; a prospect who says no shatters the closing cycle and dampens the creative spirit. A closing cycle is illustrated in Figure 6-1.

Figure 6-1

CLOSING CYCLE

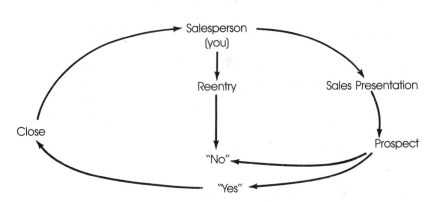

Let's analyze the components of the closing cycle (see Figure 6-2). First, the power of a successful close comes from recognizing a no response as a challenge to continue the sales presentation. Notice on the closing cycle chart that after the first no you reenter with a review of selling strong points. You assume the prospect said no because of a breakdown in communication: The prospect did not fully understand your proposition. Therefore, you counter by repeating or reviewing key points in the presentation.

Second, acknowledge all objections as legitimate problems. Find out the reason your prospect objects and express an honest concern for your prospect's feelings. *Tip:* Ask questions that appeal to the emotions. For instance, "You have a very good point, but don't you *feel*...." The word "feel" baits a prospect into giving an answer which, indeed, tells you how a prospect feels.

Third, a prospect's reluctance to say yes usually occurs for two reasons: 1) You've failed to present your proposition clearly; 2) your prospect simply can't make a decision.

Figure 6-2

COMPONENTS OF THE CLOSING CYCLE

Salesperson's Strategy	Prospect's Reaction	Salesperson's Response	Prospect's Response
Present reasons why prospect should buy.	Indicates agreement by gesture, expression, etc.	Close Sale	Buys product or service.
Presents reasons why prospect should buy now.	Indicates agreement.	Close sale	Buys product or service.
Presents reasons why prospect should buy.	No!	Reentry—come back with selling strong points.	Agrees or refuses to buy.
Reentry—repetition of selling strong points.	Introduces minor objection.	Acknowledges objection: "...an excellent point, but have you..."	Introduces still another minor objection.
Acknowledges objection: "Yes, that's true, but don't you feel..."	Agrees and doesn't register any further objections.	Attempts to close sale.	Reluctant to make a commitment. "I don't know."
Employs silence. Sees direction the presentation flows.	May raise another objection or simply say, "I really don't know."	Repeat major strong points of your presentation. Prospect may be looking for reassurance.	Says, "Do you really think this will solve my problem?"
Reassures prospect with "Yes, you'll never regret your decision to buy. It's going to save you a lot of money." Remain silent. Wait for prospect to say yes.	"Okay, you win. I'll take it!"	Close sale. Neutralize the prospect's mind.	Buys product or service.

How can you help your prospect decide? By remaining silent. Say nothing. Silence often encourages a prospect to answer his own questions and sell himself. Remember, a prospect who sells himself seldom changes his mind.

Fourth, prospects often ask questions to hear reasons why they should buy. Your answers serve to reassure them that they are making a sound decision. Here are a few typical questions:

"Do you really think this will solve my problem?"
"I just don't know when I should start the service. What do you suggest?"
"Do you think it will really save me time?"
"Don't you think the price is just a little high?"

Maintain your easygoing selling pace. Plan on closing the sale without appearing too anxious. Make it easy for the prospect to say yes.

Fifth, neutralize your prospect's mind during the close. In Chapter 3, "Cold Calling Magic in Action," you saw how the neutralization process gives you a fertile, open mind to work with. In closing the sale, you must create a pressure-free atmosphere and swing your prospect's thoughts away from the sale. Here are two ways to do this: 1) as you prepare to fill out the order pad, take your prospect's mind off the sale. Ask questions pertaining to a hobby, upcoming weekend adventure—anything other than the closing moments of your sale. 2) Keep your prospect talking about something other than your product or service. Cut in only when you need additional information for your order form. However, once you receive the information, urge your prospect to continue talking.

4. Extracting information for the big close

A big thinker extracts information from a prospect during the selling presentation to lay the groundwork for a successful close. As an example, let's follow the conversation between Carl Dober, newspaper ad salesman, and Gene Newley, sporting goods store owner.

DOBER: I've never seen so much inventory. You really have excellent merchandise, Mr. Newley.

NEWLEY: Thank you. I always try to keep a good selection, but right now things are moving slowly. My location isn't the best, you know.

DOBER: Mr. Newley, most merchants are having a tough time. Business seems down all over.

NEWLEY: Yeah, I can believe it.

DOBER: In fact, Bill Elliot of Bill's Shoes in the Palm Center has a problem very similar to yours.

NEWLEY: How so?

DOBER: Well, the Palm Center isn't located in the best part of town. So Bill ran an ad displaying the large inventory he carries. His business picked up considerably.
(Dober opens a large accordian folder)
Here, let me show you the ad we ran for Bill.

NEWLEY: (examining the ad) Oh, yes, I have seen this ad. It's clever.

DOBER: Thank you. You know, Mr. Newley, it's vitally important to promote your own business, especially in an area that is not drawing huge crowds. May I try something?

NEWLEY: (rubbing his chin) Well, I'm not sure. Just what do you have in mind?

DOBER: Let me rough out an ad, one that I know will pull for you. I'll do it tonight. Don't worry, you're under no obligation. I'll stop by tomorrow and show it to you. If you like it, we'll run the ad ... if not, you can throw it away.

NEWLEY: Fine, if you don't mind going to all the trouble.

THE NEXT MORNING ...

DOBER: Good morning, Mr. Newley. Wait'll you see what I've got.

NEWLEY: (expressing doubt) Oh ... well ... I've been thinking ...

DOBER: (quickly cuts in) Look at this ad. (Dober pulls out a sample ad) It's appealing, easy to read, and offers your customers a reasonable savings. What do you think?

NEWLEY: (slightly surprised) Hey, this is all right.

DOBER: I think so too. With thin times ahead people will be looking for ways to save money. (pointing at the ad) To attract attention, I drew a map on the botom of the ad. That'll help new customers find your store.

NEWLEY: Not bad. Do you really think it will pull?

DOBER: You bet it will. People will notice the ad and read it for sure. Let's schedule it for Wednesday, Thursday and Friday of next week, okay?

NEWLEY: How much will running the ad for three days cost me?

DOBER: Well, the timing seems right. This ad in any other newspaper would cost you over $500, but we're running a merchant's special, three runs for $278.

NEWLEY: (shaking his head) That still seems like a high price to pay.

DOBER: Believe me, Mr. Newley, this ad will really work. After all, my main concern is getting you to advertise with us regularly, not just once. If you make money with this ad, you'll run it again, won't you?

NEWLEY: Sure, if my business picks up.

DOBER: As I said earlier, Mr. Newley, during rough times people shop around looking for the best deal. Now ... are the dates for running the ad satisfactory?

NEWLEY: Yes, they're fine.

DOBER: (pulling out an order pad) What's your mailing address, Mr. Newley? Say ... I'll bet you're planning on a big weekend, aren't you?

NEWLEY: (smiling) Yeah, my wife and I are going to a play in San Francisco.

DOBER: What play are you going to see? (Dober continues to fill out the order while Mr. Newley talks about his upcoming weekend trip.)

Extracting information reveals the prospect's problems, immediate needs, and possible solutions to problems. Once a prospect exposes these concerns, a salesperson knows exactly how to set the selling scene for the closing stage. In Carl Dober's case, he offered Mr. Newley an economical way to advertise, thus attracting customers to his store.

How can you get a prospect to open up and talk to you? Here are five ways:

1. Find an interesting subject for your prospect to talk about—place of business, for example.

Carl Dober's selling picture is illustrated in Figure 6-3.

Figure 6-3

Prospect's Problems	Immediate Needs of Prospect	Possible Solutions to Problems
Sagging sales	More buying customers.	Seek ways to attract customers.
Poor business location.	More buying customers.	Move to a new location or seek ways to attract customers.
Must move large inventory.	More buying customers.	Sell merchandise.
Must advertise large inventory.	An economical way to effectively advertise large inventory.	Receive a "deal" (merchant's special) to advertise large inventory.
Questions effectiveness of running a three-day ad.	Reassurance that ad will pull in customers.	Salesperson reassures prospect through comparison (Bill's Shoes) and by stressing strong points of ad.

2. Find an outstanding feature that lends itself to conversation. Carl Dober began with, "I've never seen so much inventory."

3. Bring up challenging situations that often lead to conflict. For instance, poor business location, hard times, increased competition, and so on.

4. Let prospect know that others (suppliers, competitors, customers, etc.) are experiencing difficulties too. By making comparisons with other businesses, you encourage a

prospect to ask questions that often lead directly into your selling strong points.

5. Above all, be sympathetic and understanding. Attend to your prospect's immediate needs.

5. Turning objections into sales

A prospect may throw your timing off during the close by raising an objection. A simple objection like, "Hey, wait up. I didn't say I was going to buy" can destroy your concentration and shift the momentum away from the sale. A prospect might raise an objection to slow down the closing process. Don't let this upset you. Instead, use the objection to strengthen your close. How can you do this? First of all, don't rush your prospect with an immediate response to an objection. Listen to the objection. Then ask questions that allow your prospect to analyze his own objection and switch his thinking to buying.

As an example, let's say you're working in a jewelry store. A prospect can't decide whether or not to buy a wristwatch. Here's the conversation:

PROSPECT: (raising an objection) I don't think that I really need a new wristwatch right now.

YOU: How's your old one running? (This question puts the prospect at ease and encourages conversation.)

PROSPECT: It runs beautifully. I was just thinking about getting a little more stylish watch.

YOU: (holding up a sharp-looking watch) Do you like this one?

PROSPECT: (examines watch, looks at price tag) It's beautiful, but it's so expensive.

YOU: I can guarantee you one thing . . . (pausing for prospect to ask "what").

PROSPECT: What's that?

YOU: The price won't be going down!

PROSPECT: Yeah, I suppose you're right.

YOU: You bet. Over the past two years I've seen prices skyrocket. Look, why don't you put it on a 90-day payment program so you don't have to pay for it all at once?

PROSPECT: How much interest will I have to pay?

YOU: None. That's the best part about our 90-day program; you pay no interest at all.

PROSPECT: Well ... okay ... I'll take it.

A prospect may simply say, "No, thank you. I'm definitely not interested." A flat rejection poses a tough problem: you face the challenge of converting rejection into an objection. Why bother? A rejection builds an impregnable wall between you and your prospect; an objection leaves the door open for further negotiations.

An "absolutely not" response from a prospect can be countered with a simple "ok." After saying ok, remain silent. Prepare to leave by slowly putting away your selling materials. At this point your prospect, feeling victorious, may give reasons for rejecting your proposal. These explanations often expose the underlying objections behind the rejection. The magic of silence, in many cases, sets the selling wheels spinning again.

What if the "silent treatment" fails to evoke a response? If this happens, you might ask, "Mr. Young, what don't you like about this product?" Chances are Mr. Young will come up with the objections responsible for the rejection.

Now you're in control again. Your prospect, by revealing objections, has agreed to reconsider.

6. Closing call backs nine times out of ten

Here's a simple test item for you to think about: In most instances, if a prospect says to you, "I need time to think it over. Drop by tomorrow for my answer," you might expect:

(a) to make a sale on the following day

(b) to receive a series of stalls by the prospect

(c) to wind up without a sale

(d) to gain a customer for life

The correct answers are both b and c.

A "see you tomorrow" response usually means your prospect isn't interested in buying and wants to get rid of you. Remember, a big-thinking salesperson records sales, not stalls or rejections.

So how do you sell call backs? Begin by leaving the door open for a return visit. Don't antagonize your prospect by trying to force a decision too soon. Instead, when you return the next day, hit your prospect between the eyes with the unexpected: a new, exclusive feature you've been saving for the big finish.

For example, on your return visit on the following day, your conversation might go something like this:

PROSPECT: Gee, you know, I've been thinking. . .

YOU: (breaking in, bubbling with excitement) Mr. Hansen, I've got something that will make your day.

PROSPECT: What?

YOU: (Now's the perfect time to introduce your call back secret weapon—your product or service's strongest attribute.)

You'll dramatically increase your sales ratio on call backs if you bring an "I can't wait to see you again" attitude on your return visit. Also, shoot your veins full of enthusiasm and super saturate the selling scene with excitement.

HOW A BIG THINKER GETS THE ORDER

A big-thinking salesperson consistently combines sound planning skills with the Four Ds of salesmanship. A big thinker also programs the mind to do one thing and do it well: sell. Programming, a relatively simple task, requires you to *think* sales and prepare body processes to carry that thought into action.

Therefore, in order to sell big, you must flood your subconscious with thoughts like, "I know my prospect will buy. I've got an excellent product or service that fills a special need. I can't miss." Your entire organism, from toe to crown, will take the cue from the subconscious and behave accordingly.

A winning sales cycle emanating from the subconcious is illustrated in Figure 6-4.

Let's review the big-thinking magic important for closing sales:

1. Get in touch with your prospect's feelings. Be patient, bide your time, and prepare yourself to close when everything feels—and looks—exactly right.

2. Always expect to close the sale. A high expectancy level feeds the subconscious with happy thoughts.

Figure 6-4

WINNING SALES CYCLE

3. Give a prospect room to breathe. Don't crowd or force your prospect into making a premature decision that goes against you.

4. Don't take a no response from a prospect personally. Rather, study the components of your closing cycle. Look for a possible breakdown in communication.

5. Some prospects find the decision-making process exceedingly difficult. You can help them by outlining those benefits that will satisfy their needs.

6. Encourage a prospect to speak freely with you. Once the prospect talks, listen for cries of help.

7. Welcome objections. Treat them for what they really are: true concerns of your prospect.

8. If at first you miss a sale, return. Then catch a sale.

MAJOR PROBLEMS OF CLOSING SALES

At times closing a sale, like driving an automobile, produces stress and tension that works against you. Once you recognize these trouble spots and discover the underlying reasons for them, you can arm yourself to meet the challenge. Here are four major problems to consider:

1. Closing apathy

You might give a great presentation, but, for some reason, lose momentum as closing time nears. Again, it's a question of attitude—negataive force versus positive action.

If you feel a sale slipping away during a close, try two things: One, energize yourself by thinking of all the reasons you *must* make the sale. Your mental list might include the following:

1. A sale means a new client, a good friend.
2. This new client will direct me to other new clients.
3. A sale here will bring me one step closer to my big-thinking goal of earning $65,000 this year.
4. I have the best product or service available. My client will benefit tremendously from using it.

Two, write down your *musts* for making a sale on a 3 by 5 card. Carry the card with you. Prior to giving a selling presentation, pull out the card, read each item, and form a mental image of selling your product or service to a prospect. Repeat this procedure every time you make a selling presentation and you'll never forget your big-thinking goal and what it takes to reach it.

2. Empathizing with negative prospects

Empathy, of course, shows your concern and understanding for a prospect's dilemma. Be careful. It's easy to turn into a sponge and absorb all the woes of your prospect.

When I sold advertising space to merchants, I met many prospects who consistently dumped their problems on me. Whenever business slacked off, they would hang their heads, shrug their shoulders, and mumble sixty-three reasons why they wouldn't last out the week.

We mentioned earlier how going negative with a prospect made it easier for you to sell. That's true, but guard against your emotions taking over and gaining full control of the selling scene. A clever prospect may have you paying him to use your product or service.

You can protect yourself from negataive bombardment by playing a game called "Strainer." Think of yourself holding two strainers, one over each ear. When your prospect talks, the strainer catches the negative material and traps it; the positive information filters through with ease. In other words, you listen to only the words and sentences you wish to hear.

Another protective method is, when talking to a prospect, to look him straight in the eye and speak in a stern, sincere manner. When your prospect turns negative, focus on the bridge of his nose. This helps protect you from his gaze and minimizes the effect his voice has on you. Interestingly, at the same time, your prospect will think you're absorbing everything he says.

3. Talking too much at the close

An effective close may be as simple as "Well, Bill, that's basically it," followed by the prospect's saying, "Sounds great!"

Stop there. Say no more. You've made a sale. Now concentrate on getting specific details regarding shipment and delivery, quantity needed, size preference, and so forth.

4. Sprinting too early in the race

Getting off to a fast start puts you in the lead, but if you don't pace yourself and save the best for last, you might collapse at the finish line. So save your best shot for the close. That's the time to push your accelerator to the floor and give it all you have.

SETTING A BIG THINKER'S CLOSING PLAN INTO ACTION

What can you do to set a positive closing plan in motion? In Chapter 2 we emphasized summarizing the events of your selling presentation by recording them on a self-analysis checklist.

Here, for your convenience, is the closing section of the self-analysis checklist:

H. Closing the Sale

1. Did the prospect buy your product or service? _____

2. If "yes," did the sale come early in the presentation? _____

3. Was the sale a relatively easy one? _____

4. If you didn't clinch the sale, why do you think the prospect didn't buy? _____

   _____

5. How many trial closes did you make? _____ How did the prospect respond to these closes? _____

6. After testing the sales climate with trial closes, how many times did you attempt to close? _____

7. At the end of each close did you carefully observe your prospect's reactions? _____

8. After your first close what did the prospect say and how did he react? The prospect said _____

   _____

   The prospect reacted by _____

   _____

9. How much pressure or tension was present during the close? _____

10. What did you do to ease the situation? _____

11. How do you honestly feel about your close? _____

   _____

After making a selling presentation and filling out the closing section of the self-analysis checklist, you'll uncover the areas that need remediation.

Let's say, for example, that your answers to Items 8, 9 and 11 came out like this:

8. After your first close what did the prospect say and how did he react? The prospect said *No, he wasn't interested at this time.*

The prospect reacted *by saying he could get along without the product. He turned and walked away.*

9. How much pressure or tension was present during the close? *Prospect restless and unfriendly.*

11. How do you honestly feel about your close? *It was tense and uncomfortable for everyone.*

Now's the time to check your Weekly Tally Card (Chapter 2) and review the closing problems which exist. An example of how your card might appear is shown in Figure 6-5.

Figure 6-5

**SELF-ANALYSIS CHECKLIST
WEEKLY TALLY CARD**

Week Number: <u>6</u>   From: <u>2/5</u> To: <u>2/9</u>

Closing the Sale

41 presentations—16 sales; 25 no sales.

Problems

1. Trying too hard to sell; much too eager.
2. Not spending enough time establishing a comfortable selling situation.

Outline your strategy for improving your closing style on the back of the card. An example is shown in Figure 6-6.

Figure 6-6

REMEDIATION

1. Emphasize front talk. Loosen up and get to know your prospect.
2. Remind yourself *why* you must make the sale. Refer to mental *must* list for selling.
3. Take time to extract information from your prospect.

Constantly review your self-analysis checklist. Go through the weekly tally cards. Rid your selling presentation of weak spots and continually seek to make each successive close stronger than the previous one.

POINTS TO REMEMBER

As a big thinker you spend hours putting together a selling program destined for success. The key parts must mesh together and run smoothly at all times.

Your closing power dictates, for the most part, how long your selling machine will function in an effective manner. The critical parts that determine your closing success are: 1) your ability to practice patience and study the individual mannerisms of each prospect; 2) your desire to come up winners; 3) your skill at using the components of the closing cycle to your advantage; 4) your ability to extract valuable information from a prospect; 5) your skill at handling call backs; 6) your ability to turn objections into sales; and 7) your willingness to evaluate your progress and seek steps to strengthen your total selling program.

CHAPTER SEVEN

SELLING BIG WITH THE MAGIC OF HUMOR

David Seabury said, "Good humor isn't a trait of character, it is an art that requires practice." Every big-thinking salesperson should post this quotation in a conspicuous place. These powerful words suggest the importance of including humor as you present your product or service.

A word of caution: Not every person laughs at the same thing or confesses to having a good sense of humor. Therefore, it takes insight, keen observational powers, and wisdom to know exactly when and when not to employ levity in a selling situation.

The following areas will be covered in this chapter:

1. How the magic of humor adds zest to your sales presentation
2. Does your prospect have a sense of humor? (a test)
3. Ways to make your prospect laugh
4. Injecting humor throughout your sales presentation
5. Setting the limits on humor
6. Knowing when not to be funny
7. Using humor to sell your product or service
8. How humor improves your selling performance
9. Where to find humorous ideas to increase your sales

Now let's see how humor can help you to reach your big-thinking objective.

1. HOW THE MAGIC OF HUMOR ADDS ZEST TO YOUR SALES PRESENTATION

As you know, a sense of humor is one of the most personable traits a person can have. Tasteful humor can turn an ordinary moment into an exciting event. And if you allow humor to flow at its own pace, your sales presentation will pick up momentum and capture the enthusiasm of your prospect. Here are five ways in which humor gives your sales presentation a lift:

One, it puts you and your prospect at ease. When you recognize a humorous situation and respond by smiling or commenting on the occasion, your prospect tends to relax and pay more attention to what you have to say. This, in turn, bolsters your selling confidence. So it follows that an attentive prospect is more likely to buy your product or service than one who fails to respond.

Avoid spiking your sales presentation with "ready-made" humor—that is, stale jokes or so-called hilarious situations that occurred "just last month." The best humor evolves spontaneously and takes everyone by surprise. These are unplanned moments when your demonstration sputters or something unexpected happens or a spoken word trips and stumbles across your lips.

Two, it allows your prospect to open up and become more receptive to your ideas. Often a humorous incident sets your prospect loose on a "that reminds me" tangent. Fine. Give your prospect room to reminisce and have fun. Pay close attention to what your prospect says and reinforce the situation by showing genuine enthusiasm. If you convince your prospect that you're truly interested in him, he'll reciprocate by showing an interest in you and your product or service.

Three, it gives you total control of the selling situation. A tense prospect, for example, may feel uneasy and find it difficult to concentrate. A lighthearted approach invites your prospect to loosen up, listen, and ask questions. As a big thinker you determine the flow and direction your sales presentation takes. Therefore, the magic of humor comes from your ability to quickly assess a prospect's personality and adjust your sales presentation accordingly.

Four, it creates a common bond between you and your

prospect. Humor brings people together and allows them to share interesting experiences. It takes a sensitive, understanding salesperson to enjoy the humorous story of a prospect without trying to "go one better." A smart salesperson allows the prospect free rein to tell a story without interruption.

Five, it keeps you and your prospect in a positive frame of mind. Humor is fun, and when you are having a good time selling becomes a happy challenge.

2. DOES YOUR PROSPECT HAVE A SENSE OF HUMOR? (A TEST)

There is a big difference between having a sense of humor and being in a laughing mood. A prospect, for instance, may have received some distressing news moments before your arrival. Your prospect, driven to anger, may snap at you and smother any notion of creating a humorous setting. Now this doesn't mean your prospect lacks a sense of humor; it simply reveals this isn't the time to go for laughs.

Here's a five-item test to help you determine if your prospect has a sense of humor:

1. After introducing yourself, lead off with "I hope I caught you on a buying day" or "My horoscope said that today would be a big day for me. Do you read your horoscope?" Carefully observe your prospect's reaction. This will give you a fair indication of what to expect during your sales presentation.

2. A prospect reveals, through facial expressions and tone of voice, the role humor plays in various situations. So as you carry on a casual conversation, pay close attention to the stimuli that put a smile on your prospect's face. Take mental notes and try to include similar stimuli in your sales presentation.

3. Start a conversation with an amusing anecdote, something that happened between you and a prospect. Try to relate these circumstances to the present situation. If your story misses its mark, try again. Be careful. An apathetic response from your prospect may be a signal for you to skip the levity.

4. Simply ask your prospect straightforward questions about his family, hobby, recreational interests, business, and so forth. As your prospect talks, look for clues that indicate what events stimulate your prospect's funny bone.

5. Center your humor around your prospect; that is, present a humorous incident or expression in a manner that requires your prospect to respond. For example, "Mr. Singer, how would you have handled that situation?" or "Ms. Trimble, have you ever experienced anything so bizarre?" Again, let your prospect's reaction be a tip-off for things to come.

In summary, your best guide for determining a prospect's temperament or degree of humor is to test it by presenting humorous situations that require a response from your prospect. How your prospect reacts will give you a clear picture of what to expect.

3. WAYS TO MAKE YOUR PROSPECT LAUGH

You don't have to be a stand-up comedian and feed your prospect a volley of one-liners to make sales. In fact, if you go overboard to be funny, your prospect may feel that your product or service is also a joke, or that you're using humor to hide something.

The idea, of course, is to get your prospect to laugh with you, not become suspicious of your motives. This free-flowing humor should occur naturally and be a byproduct of conversation between you and your prospect. Remember, a contented prospect is more receptive to buying your product or service. As an example, Ron Manning worked with me selling advertising a few years back. He took selling seriously, yet he consistently recorded low sales. His problem revolved around a stale presentation devoid of humor. It came off cold and stilted. According to Ron, his prospects quickly lost interest and invented excuses to "leave and go about their business."

I assisted Ron by showing him ways to liven up his sales presentation. Within six months his sales volume increased more than 50 percent, and his annual earnings shot up over $16,000. The following example shows how Ron uses humor in his sales presentation:

RON: What's the one thing that bothers you the most about advertising?

PROSPECT: (with a slight chuckle) Heck, you don't know if it works!

RON: You're 100 percent correct. That's why I'm going to ask you for a check now, and you can forget the ad, okay? (prospect laughs)

RON: Well, at least you know up front that you're not getting your money's worth, right?

PROSPECT: Gosh, I hope I do. (Prospect laughs and shakes his head). You're the first honest ad person I've run into.

This question-asking technique encourages the prospect to open up and reveal a major concern: not being able to evaluate the effectiveness of advertising.

Again, the magic of making humor work rests with common sense. If your prospect isn't in the mood to laugh, don't press it. Conversely, if your prospect wishes to continue this light repartee, relax and have fun. If the humor begins to fade, then go right into your sales presentation.

Another area that lends itself to humor is price. In many instances when a salesperson mentions price, the prospect assumes a defensive stance and waits for the bomb to drop. This need not happen if you avoid mentioning price during your sales presentation. The time to talk price (and toss in a slice of humor) is when you finish your sales presentation. It works like this:

YOU: Well, that's it, Ms. Davies. Do you have any questions?

MS. DAVIES: One big one: How much is this going to cost me?

YOU: I never thought you'd ask ... the price is really the best part.

MS. DAVIES: For you maybe, but not for me.

YOU: That's where you're wrong, Ms. Davies. Honestly, the price *is* the best part.

This cat and mouse strategy gives both you and your prospect a chance to inject humor. Keep in mind that your prospect's mood, attitude, and patience determine how successful you will be.

These two examples point up a significant factor when dealing with humor: Often the biggest question in the mind of a prospect becomes the launching pad for humorous conversation.

4. INJECTING HUMOR THROUGHOUT YOUR SALES PRESENTATION

We said earlier that you can't tell for sure what your prospect will find amusing. The best humor, as you know, develops spontaneously, often without warning. A big-thinking salesperson keeps a sharp eye out for anything that can be readily used before, during, and after a sales presentation.

Let's examine four ways to inject humor throughout your sales presentation.

One, when you feel the timing is right, bring up how a past blunder put you at the mercy of your prospect. As an example, the time your attache case flew open and papers scattered about, or when you bent over to pick up a pencil and ripped out the seat of your pants. A prospect will admire your honesty in exposing yourself (no pun intended) as a vulnerable human being.

Two, bait your prospect into asking you for an amusing anecdote. Let's say, for instance, you are talking with Barbara Keeting, business manager for Donna Paper Products. The conversation might go something like this:

Ms. KEETING: Your proposal sounds interesting, but I'm still not completely convinced.

YOU: That's understandable, Ms. Keeting. In fact, Mr. Russell, the sales manager for Alliance Chemicals, said practically the same thing last year.

(You smile and shake your head.) It was funny what happened.

Ms. KEETING: What?

Another example:

YOU: Well, what do you think, Ms. Keeting? Are you interested?

Ms. KEETING: I'm not sure. I'll need more time to consider your proposal.

YOU: Fine, but be careful! Don't let what happened to Mr. Russell, the sales manager for Alliance Chemicals, happen to you.

Ms. KEETING: What?

Make sure you have an amusing story ready to go. You'd look foolish and risk losing a sale if you couldn't produce a timely anecdote.

Three, if your prospect says or does something funny, reinforce the behavior by highlighting the moment; that is, you might say, "Funny comment. I'll have to remember that one," or "Hey, that's great. Let me see you do it again."

Four, refer to your prospect's humorous incident whenever it's proper to do so during your sales presentation. It shows a definite interest in your prospect as a person first, possible sale second.

Final point: Don't take yourself, your prospect, or your product or service too seriously. Be honest and straightforward in your approach, but stay on the lookout for an opportunity to sneak in a bit of humor.

5. SETTING THE LIMITS ON HUMOR

As a big thinker you learn through careful observation and experience just how far to go with humor. You soon recognize which areas or subjects are most likely to offend rather than amuse prospects. And you realize that it's the prospect, not the salesperson, who should set the pace for humor.

The following guidelines will serve as reminders to help you keep your selling approach on track.

1. Allow humor to flow as a natural part of your personality. Refrain from trying to be funny. Forced humor comes off stilted and encourages your prospect to doubt your selling ability.

2. Keep humorous stories short and go easy on detail. Long, drawn-out anecdotes tend to bore prospects, especially if they are not personally involved or know the people you are describing.

3. Keep from laughing too much or at everything your prospect says or does. Too much of anything wears thin in a hurry.

4. Concentrate on good clean humor. Stay away from political, religious, or ethnic references. You could lose a potential sale by making an "innocent" comment that ruffles the feathers of your prospect. As an example, a salesman friend of mine lost a sale for making the following comment regarding California politics:

> It only took Jerry four years to tear down what it took Reagan eight years to build.

My friend should have known better. You don't make cutting remarks about a democratic leader to a staunch democrat. How would my friend know that his prospect was a die-hard democrat? In most cases, he wouldn't know unless the prospect, for some reason, mentioned this beforehand. Therefore, why take a chance? Political opinions are nothing more than personal feelings. And in the case of politics, those feelings are best kept locked inside.

5. Refrain from making off-color or derogatory remarks about others, especially prospects and competitors. Few prospects are impressed when they hear demeaning comments such as "I met a prospect last month who wasn't wrapped too tight," or "Anybody who would buy from them should have a brain scan." Trying to draw laughs at the expense of others shows a lack of good sense, compassion, and professionalism. Also, these comments raise a question in the mind of a prospect: What does he *really* think about me?

6. Be yourself. Don't model your behavior after Steve Martin, Bill Cosby, or Don Rickles. It'll come off as a fourth-rate imitation and show you as having little or no imagination. The best way to turn off a prospect is by trying to be something or somebody you're not.

6. KNOWING WHEN NOT TO BE FUNNY

There are times when humor acts like a deadly poison and kills any chances of closing a sale. A big-thinking salesperson learns early to recognize these situations and avoids them at all costs. Let's examine four of these critical areas.

One, when something happens during a sales presentation that changes the conversation from a light to a serious tone, check out the circumstances before attempting humor. Pay particular attention to your prospect's verbal and facial expressions, since they provide clues that tell you what direction to take. You can't be absolutely certain what created the mood change, so you'd be smart not to rely on humor to restore order.

Two, if you're unsure whether or not to employ humor, pretend for the moment that you *are* the prospect. Now ask yourself, "Is this a good time for levity?" If your answer comes up no, then skip the humor and wait for a more convenient time.

Three, if there is no definite advantage for you or your prospect to engage in humor, try something else. In fact, your best bet at this particular time might be to present a serious, straightforward sales presentation.

Four, when in doubt about how your prospect feels or thinks regarding a person, place, or thing, don't call upon humor to find out. You may find yourself with one less prospect.

Remember, it pays to use humor wisely and only when it fits the present situation. Therefore, a rule of thumb is: Let your prospect lead the way.

7. USING HUMOR TO SELL YOUR PRODUCT OR SERVICE

Without question, humor can help you reach your major selling objective if you use it as a selling tool, not as a vehicle to collect a few random laughs.

An excellent time to add humor is when your prospect runs away with the conversation and you wish to gain control again. As soon as your prospect pauses for a gulp of air, inject a small dose of humor. Try to weave the humor around the thoughts of your prospect. Let your comment gradually slip into the conversation. After you release your comment, pause and wait for your prospect's reaction. If your prospect laughs, join in on the laughter. If your prospect fails to laugh or looks at you as if you're crazy, don't become discouraged. Some prospects are so absorbed in their own thoughts that they don't return to earth until their fuel supply runs low. But stick with it. Sooner or later you'll be directing traffic and running the show once more.

Another good time to slip in humor is during a serious presentation. Even if you're selling the greatest product or service in the world, it's imperative that you add just enough humor to break up the monotony. Fatigue destroys enthusiasm; fading enthusiasm leads to a condition known as "Prospectus goodbyus." Translation: Sorry no sale.

No matter how you choose to use humor, keep one thought in mind: Levity will work in your favor if you combine the felicities of empathy, sensitivity, and intelligence.

8. HOW HUMOR IMPROVES YOUR SELLING PERFORMANCE

Humor is a personality trait (or personable art) that most people admire. In fact, when you use humor in a sensible and genuine way, you improve your selling performance in the following seven ways.

One, you convey a simple message to your prospect: I like selling and I enjoy talking with you. Your prospect, in turn, signals acceptance by responding in a positive manner.

Two, your listening skills improve because you mentally search for spots in a conversation to insert a humorous anecdote or two.

Three, humor puts both you and your prospect in high spirits. It often provides the lift necessary to get your prospect to think seriously about your proposal.

Four, a prospect who laughs with you and enjoys your humor is most likely to believe in you and your product or service.

Five, when times get tough humor often provides a crutch to lean on until things improve. Raymond Hitchcock said, "A man isn't poor if he can still laugh."

Six, it enables you to think clearly and remain alert. Humor, as stated earlier, reduces stress and tension, thus providing a relaxed atmosphere.

Seven, humor is just plain fun. It gives you a chance to be creative in your selling approach.

Humor, then, can be a good friend and lead you toward bigger and better sales when handled properly.

9. WHERE TO FIND HUMOROUS IDEAS TO INCREASE YOUR SALES

In a word, everywhere. Yes, ideas spring up when you least expect them, and often in places where you might never think to look. Naturally, when a humorous idea strikes—particularly one that fits your selling repertoire—you savor it like a last bite of delicious candy.

Where are some productive places to search for ideas? The following ten suggestions will give you a start:

1. Study the newspaper, especially the human interest section. Often these stories contain humorous anecdotes that can enter the casual conversation or front talk phase of your sales presentation.

2. Attend social gatherings such as special meetings, banquets, club get-togethers, and parties. Listen to what others are saying. Join the group that seems to be having the most fun. Find out what topics bring the biggest laughs. Then extract those key items and make them part of your selling arsenal.

3. Listen to the radio. Concentrate on how radio announcers or disk jockeys use humor to stimulate the interest of their listeners. For example, after listening to a witty monologue or funny story, ask yourself: Why did these articles amuse me? Write your answers on a piece of paper. Now see if you can fit these items into your sales presentation.

4. Watch several television programs. Select one or two sit-coms and extract the elements which, in your opinion, account for their success. Again, try to include these key elements in your selling approach.

5. Read humor books and magazines. Study the techniques these authors use to generate laughter in their readers.

6. Attend workshops and lectures. Invariably the speakers who build a reputation for being "funny and witty" draw the largest crowds. Watch these people work. Study how the audience reacts. Before long you'll discover the magic or charisma that pulls everything together. Often it's just a matter of pinpointing how a speaker talks or moves about the platform or speaks directly to the audience, and so on.

7. Draw from your own personal experiences; that is, think about one or two humorous incidents. When the situation presents itself, insert the "triggers" or "motivators" that set them off.

8. Surround yourself with funny people—those capable of making others laugh and feel good about themselves. In many cases, humorous people are also positive thinkers.

9. Ask others what they think makes a situation funny. Talk to fellow salespeople about their funniest experience. Chances are you'll pick up a clue or tip that will come in handy later on.

10. Ask youself: What occurs during a selling situation that makes me laugh? Often the answer to this question reveals how you feel about your product or service, prospect, and yourself. So if you're using humor to help build your sales, you should reach your selling objective in a delightful way.

POINTS TO REMEMBER

What's funny? Just about anything that makes people laugh. And since prospects are people, they respond favorably to humor, especially if it's delivered in good taste.

A big-thinking salesperson combines intelligence, insight, and common sense to create the right moment or situation for humor.

You must "size up" your prospect before employing humor. Some prospects aren't impressed with amusing stories or light-hearted conversation.

Humor should be a natural, free-flowing experience that both you and your prospect can enjoy. Don't overload or oversell a humorous incident. Keep anecdotes short and to the point.

Test your prospect's mood and attitude before attempting humor. A grouchy prospect can knock the stuffing out of your sales presentation.

How far should you go with humor? As far as you like, but allow intelligent observation and experience to help you make a wise decision.

Remember, it's your prospect who sets the pace for humor. Therefore, relax. Have fun. Smile. Then sell, sell, sell.

CHAPTER EIGHT

RECOGNIZING AND SOLVING MAJOR SELLING PROBLEMS

As a big-thinking salesperson you'll face numerous obstacles and danger zones famous for stalling the selling machine. Obviously these roadblocks retard your climb to the top. Therefore, the length of time it takes you to reach the summit depends on your ability to solve each problem.

In this section we'll examine 15 major problems and practical suggestions for solving them. Here are the 15 problem areas:

1. Holding a narrow-minded view of yourself or your prospect
2. Staying within your comfort zone
3. Trying to do too much too soon
4. Working without written goals
5. Listening to negative self-talk
6. Talking too much, listening too little
7. Missing your prospect's viewpoint
8. Sidestepping your prospect's interest
9. Failing to interest your prospect
10. Letting enthusiasm die and wither away
11. Allowing prospect to slip away
12. Failing to help prospect solve problem
13. Overloading your sales presentation
14. Neglecting to stress major points in your selling presentation
15. Neglecting to allow prospect to sell himself

Now let's review each item and see how to correct the situation.

1. HOLDING A NARROW-MINDED VIEW
OF YOURSELF OR YOUR PROSPECT

Narrow-mindedness thrives on such words as "limited" and "restricted." These words suggest that you can only go so far. Once you reach this mental barrier, the trip ends and it's time to begin over again or try something new.

These "negatrons" of failure express themselves in the following manner:

A: I can't sell Mr. Fernly. He's too much like my high school English teacher.

B: Ms. Wiggins has no sense of humor. I'm wasting my time with her.

C: Hey, Ron said that Mr. Daniels hates salespeople. So I'm scratching him off my prospect list.

D: I've tried twice to sell Ms. Crane. Why go for a third turndown?

E: If I can sell two prospects today, I'll be satisfied.

In Figure 8-1 we take a closer look at each statement and see how narrow-mindedness limits progress.

As you can see, the foundation for housing narrow-minded views comes from negative past experiences, heresay, insufficient information, lack of drive, and self-limits.

In the *Big Thinker's Positive Statements* column you'll find clues for eliminating "negatrons." They are as follows:

- Recognizing the problem. For example, "Mr. Fernly is a tough prospect" or "Ms. Wiggins is a serious person."

- Preparing to meet the problem squarely. For example, "I'm determined to sell...." or "I'll give her a first-rate sales presentation."

- Anticipating a successful outcome. For example, "Selling him will be quite a feat" or "I'll present my product and myself in a confident way."

So in order to prevent narrow thinking from sweeping your sales presenation, do three things: One, stay on the lookout for problems; two, once you identify a conflict area, attack the problem immediately; and three, expect and accept nothing less than success.

Figure 8-1

Negative Statements	"Negatrons"	Criterion For Judgment	Big Thinker's Positive Statements
"I can't sell Mr. Fernly. He's too much like my high school English teacher."	Can't; too much like...(negative comparison)	Evident reminder of bad past experience.	"Mr. Fernly is a tough prospect. Selling him will be quite a feat."
"Ms. Wiggins has no sense of humor. I'm wasting my time with her."	Has no...; wasting my time...	Bases success of sale on only one character trait.	"Ms. Wiggins is a serious person. I'll give her a first-rate sales presentation."
"Hey, Ron said that Mr. Daniels hates salespeople. I'm scratching him off my prospect list."	Hates salespeople; scratching him off...	Strictly heresay.	"I'll present my product and myself in a confident way. I'm looking forward to meeting Mr. Daniels."
"I've tried twice to sell Ms. Crane. Why go for a third turndown?"	Why try?	Two successive failures indicate no hope.	"I'm determined to sell Ms. Crane a valuable service."
"If I can sell two prospects today, I'll be satisfied."	Limitation	Success quota	"I'll try to sell as many prospects as I possibly can."

2. STAYING WITHIN YOUR COMFORT ZONE

It's tough to leave a warm, cozy house when it's cold and windy outside. It puts a mental and physical strain on your body. Your comfort zone, like the warm, cozy house, offers you a safe, secure selling environment. It works like this: As long as you avoid taking a risk—that is, making the sacrifices necessary to triple your yearly income, you needn't worry about failure.

Why are salespeople reluctant to leave their comfort zone? For some it's simply a matter of self-expectancy. They see themselves earning X dollars a year and there's no reason for anticipating a double or triple jump in the near future. After all, nobody (including themselves) expects them to earn anything more than a moderate income.

A salesperson who appears perfectly happy earning a modest salary may balk at leaving his comfort zone. There are several reasons for this: One, he may fear that sudden success will drive envious friends away; two, his selling style may change from a nonchalant, low-key approach to a pushy, aggressive role; three, he may think that he'll be deserting those less ambitious than himself; and four, he just can't see himself earning a high income. In fact, if his earning power raises significantly, he panics and feels anxious until things return to normal again.

As a big thinker you can't afford to take refuge in your comfort zone. Once you decide to double or triple your earning power, your comfort zone will no longer exist. It'll dissolve like an Alka Seltzer tablet in a glass of lukewarm water. This is perhaps the toughest thing you'll ever have to do. Your comfort zone won't lay down and die; it will cry out like a cat with a sore paw. Case in point: Brian S., a used car salesman, earned approximately $2,000 a month selling cars. In one eight-day period last fall he earned $850. Did this windfall give him an incentive to shoot for record sales? No. He decided to take a week off because, according to Brian, "I'm eight days ahead of myself." In other words, Brian allowed his comfort zone to control the amount of money he earned each month.

What can you do to keep from falling into the comfort zone trap? Here are five suggestions:

1. As your earnings increase, continue to assess your total selling approach. Build on your strengths while you correct your

weaknesses. You can do this by reviewing your Master Selling Plan, especially your goal statements and how you intend to reach these goals. Let your Master Selling Plan serve as a constant reminder to keep pushing forward.

2. If you double or triple your earnings ahead of schedule, shoot for higher stakes. For instance, if you plan to double your income within six months and you reach your objective in three months, don't say to yourself, "Hey, now I can coast for the next three months. I'm ahead in the game." Let the Brians of the world ride this attitude into the depths of the comfort zone.

3. Remember, goals are like steps in a ladder. They provide realistic targets but should be flexible enough to keep pace with your selling progress. Therefore, if your goals become obsolete due to your accelerated efforts, simply update them.

4. Read and study your daily affirmations. Put them into practice.

5. Study your Self-Analysis Checklist. Know at all times what parts of your selling plan are responsible for your progress or lack of progress.

3. TRYING TO DO TOO MUCH TOO SOON

Some sales people make the mistake of activating monster goals around a "hurry up" selling plan. In short, they try to reap high rewards in record-breaking time. When they fail, the pilot light flickers and finally dies. This opens the door for a condition known as selling burnout (Chapter 10). It's like a runner who after only two weeks of training attempts to break a track record. The machine just isn't ready to meet the challenge.

Pacing, then, acts as a magical ingredient to point your selling progress in a steady, upward direction. Pacing keeps you on schedule, synchronizes your efforts with your selling plan, and allows you to expend energy in a positive way.

So in order to avoid spreading your selling efforts too thin, try these suggestions:

1. Have a daily written plan ready to go. Make a do-it-now priority list. Put the most important item first on the list.

2. Keep your list challenging but within reason. If you find that you've overloaded your day, omit an activity or two. Remember, there's always tomorrow.

3. Practice patience. In most cases a healthy attitude coupled with hard work spawns excellent results. You'll reach your big-thinking objective within your allotted time if you plan wisely, seek steady improvement, and believe in yourself.

4. WORKING WITHOUT WRITTEN GOALS

By now you're fully aware of how written goals give your selling program purpose and direction. You also realize how written goals keep you on target, act as motivational devices, and provide a sound foundation for assessing your effectiveness as a big-thinking salesperson. Clearly, the thought of working without written goals would be like driving a car at night with no lights.

Yet some salespeople continue to operate on a day-to-day basis without any specific guidelines. They gauge success by the number of sales made that day. This method, of course, is short-lived, and seldom yields anything but frustration for the salesperson.

Admittedly, there are salespeople who create their own system of getting goals, which often excludes writing everything down on paper. As an example, Cindy Nicholson, an insurance agent from Long Beach, California, earns $35,000 to $40,000 a year using a four-part selling format for meeting her major objective. Her plan includes the following:

1. Every morning Ms. Nicholson repeats her major selling objective to herself several times.

2. Then she asks herself, "What must I do today to help me reach my major selling objective?"

3. She records information on a selling log sheet after meeting with each prospect. Here's a copy of her sheet:

SELLING LOG SHEET

1. Date _____

2. Prospect's Name _____

3. Prospect's Address _____

4. Name of Business _____

5. Meeting Time _____

6. Length of Meeting _____

7. Overall Review of Meeting

   a. What was the selling scene like? _____

   _____

   _____

   _____

   b. Describe prospect's general behavior toward presentation.

   _____

   c. What positive events transpired during the meeting? _____

   _____

   d. What negative events transpired during the meeting? _____

   _____

   e. What must I do to improve my selling technique?

   _____

   _____

   _____

   f. What were the results of the meeting?

      1. Prospect definitely not interested in policy. _____

      2. Prospect not interested at this time. Try again later on.

      _____

      3. Prospect shows signs of interest. Should purchase policy
         on return visit. _____

      4. Prospect purchased policy during meeting. _____

8. Additional comments: _____

   _____

4. At the end of the day Ms. Nicholson reviews her log sheets. She concentrates on Items 7c, 7d, and 7e. She claims Item 7e is the driving force behind her success.

Select any method you wish for meeting your major selling objective. The important thing to remember is: find a workable plan, then plan the work.

5. LISTENING TO NEGATIVE SELF-TALK

Negative self-talk is the inner conversation you have with yourself which revolves around such expressions as "I can't sell him because..." or "There is no way..." or "It's a waste of time to..." And so on. Often these negative views serve as defense mechanisms to reduce anxiety or to deny or distort the truth. They may arise during pressure moments or when sales slow down.

We discussed earlier in the book how "negative creepers" can sneak up on you and invade your sales presentation. Unfortunately, it takes less effort to hide behind a defense mechanism than to seek out the trouble spots and eliminate them.

The true test of a big thinker comes when hard times stimulate the flow of negative self-talk and forces the salesperson to make a decision—either respond in a negative manner or concentrate solely on a positive solution.

These suggestions will help you handle conflicts and problems without falling into the negative trap.

1. Anticipate areas where problems are likely to occur, then prepare yourself to handle them should they arise.
2. Face the problem squarely. Don't look for alibis or excuses to smooth things over.
3. Look for an immediate solution to the problem. The longer you wait, the harder it becomes to solve the problem.
4. If necessary, ask for assistance. Coordinating efforts to tackle a problem shows good sense.

5. Never give up. Face each conflict as a personal challenge.

6. Picture yourself in a positive light. Visualize working with friendly prospects who have a definite need for your product or service.

7. Look forward to meeting new, exciting prospects each day. Feel good about what you are doing.

6. TALKING TOO MUCH, LISTENING TOO LITTLE

Some salespeople are bitten by the "Me talk, you listen" bug. They become so impressed with the sound of their own voices that the opinions and statements of others, namely prospects, fall on deaf ears.

Talkers are notorious for driving prospects away. As an example, Ken S. worked with me a few years ago selling newspaper advertising in Grass Valley, California. Ken started out with a big thinker's philosophy but lasted approximately eight months. He had a bad habit of asking a question and answering it himself. This, of course, aggravated his prospects.

I covered Ken's territory after he left. Some of his prospects would describe him as the guy who could "talk the ears off a rabbit." Clearly, a person can't effectively talk and listen at the same time, especially if he's trying to sell a prospect.

It follows, then, that if you listen intently to what your prospect says, you greatly increase your chances of making a sale for these reasons:

1. A prospect feels important, his ego expands, and he becomes easier to manage.

2. You learn what your prospect finds pleasurable and annoying. You, therefore, can adjust your sales presentation to the whims of your prospect.

3. You discover the prospect's needs without having to make wild guesses or assumptions.

4. As mentioned earlier, a good listener is often tagged an intelligent conversationalist.

5. A careful listener shows patience and understanding.

These traits, in turn, signal the prospect that his thoughts and ideas are highly regarded.

7. MISSING YOUR PROSPECT'S VIEWPOINT

You can best understand a prospect if you know his point of view; that is, how he feels about his situation at the present time. You may find out by asking pertinent questions and listening to the answers. This seems painfully easy, yet some salespeople lose their prospects early in a sales presentation because they neglect to "size up the selling situation."

Avoid smothering your prospect with stories about you, your company, or your product or service. Get your prosepct to talk about himself and his problems. After your prospect reveals his wants and needs, you can show him exactly how you and your company may help.

Two methods of interpersonal communication which will help you understand your prospect's viewpoint are paraphrasing and perception check.

In paraphrasing, you repeat in your own words what you heard your prospect say. Then you check with your prospect to be sure you accurately understood. For example:

PROSPECT: I might be interested in your service if I could be sure it would increase sales.

YOU: Am I correct in assuming you want proof that our service will boost your profits?

In perception checking, you transform your prospect's expression of feeling into a tentative description of feeling by asking if you have understood the feeling expressed. For example:

PROSPECT: Hell, every time I run an ad this time of year, it doesn't draw flies.

YOU: You feel that running an ad right now is a waste of time and money, don't you?

These two techniques increase your listening skills and convince a prospect that you understand his dilemma and empathize with him.

8. SIDESTEPPING YOUR PROSPECT'S INTEREST

A salesperson may innocently circumvent a prospect's interest in favor of highlighting his own product or service. A disgruntled prospect, feeling less than adequate, may respond by rejecting the salesperson's proposal.

First impressions mean everything to some people. A wise salesperson knows this and makes a quick study of every prospect in order to determine what things are held in high regard. Once a prospect feels confident that you share his interest, you become a significant figure of authority. The prospect believes that you are the right person to service his needs.

Your big-thinking task is to coax your prospect into revealing his special interests. Once you learn what they are, you will be in a position to control the selling scene. You can do this simply by letting your prospect talk. As he talks, take mental notes on those items that make your prospect laugh or react in an energetic fashion. When this moment arrives, ask questions to show you are interested in what your prospect is saying. With few exceptions, you become an interesting person in the eyes of your prospect. Prospects like to deal with interesting people.

9. FAILING TO INTEREST YOUR PROSPECT

When you fail to interest your prospect you inevitably lose a sale. It's discouraging to write "prospect not interested" on a sale report. That statement alone suggests that the prospect wasn't ready to buy or the prospect wasn't impressed with your product or service or the prospect didn't feel comfortable with you.

But why wouldn't a prospect feel comfortable with you? You are sincere, energetic, and ambitious, aren't you? Well, to be honest, some salespeople bore their prospects by talking too much about too little. In other words, they dominate a conversation by pounding on a subject that holds little or no interest for the prospect. Take, as an example, a salesperson who talks about the "good old days" when he was a star player on his college baseball team. He rattles on about his throwing and hitting ability. Unless the prospect is a nostalgia buff, the salesperson will strike out before coming to home plate.

In order to keep your prospect alert and ready to buy, employ the following suggestions:

One, present yourself in an appealing manner. Smile, be happy, and enjoy the time you spend with your prospect. When you do, a warm, glowing sensation wells up inside of you like magma brewing within a volcanic chamber. Before long it rises to the surface, spews out, and touches everything in its path.

Two, keep an open mind. You don't have to agree with everything a prospect says, but don't be in a hurry to disagree either. When in doubt, say nothing.

Three, stay abreast of what's going on in the world. You should have a superficial knowledge of many subjects—just enough information so you can carry on an intelligent conversation with your prospect. It has been said that a little knowledge is a dangerous thing, but in the selling game no knowledge at all often results in "prospect not interested."

10. LETTING ENTHUSIASM DIE AND WITHER AWAY

Is it possible for salespeople who lack polish and selling experience to succeed in selling? Yes, if they generate enthusiasm in everything they do. Sadly, some salespeople settle for satisfaction, never wishing to leave their comfort zone. After a period of time, boredom enters, lethargy takes over, and symptoms of selling burnout sneak in the back door.

Enthusiasm is a combination of several things, but the two most important ingredients are emotion and energy. Enthusiasm builds an intensity that creates a deep, positive impression on the prospect. This energy release spreads like rumors in a gossip section. An enthusiastic selling approach can capture a prospect's interest and take his mind off of business worries long enough to see how your product or service can meet his immediate needs. Clearly, enthusiasm commands attention.

Enthusiasm sells tough prospects. Bob Chandler sold newspaper advertising to prospects in a rural community in northern California. Bob told me that the make or break part of his selling presentation often came when the prospect said, "No, I don't need your service." At this point pressure builds for both prospect and salesperson. "You'd like to grab your case and run," said Bob. "But here's where you must turn the enthusiastic dial to full power."

Here's an example of how Bob's enthusiasm and perseverance help win sales:

MR. JAMES (PROSPECT): Really, I'm just not in the market to advertise in your newspaper.

BOB: Okay, Mr. James, that's your decision. However, let me ask you this: Since you're a responsible businessman, isn't it important for you to get the most circulation for the least amount of advertising dollars?

MR. JAMES: Well, of course.

BOB: Then let me assure you that I'll do everything in my power to make that happen. After all, we do have the largest circulation in the area.

MR. JAMES: Yeah, but no one reads your newspaper!

BOB: Actually, Mr. James, they really do. In fact, I'll tell you what. Let's run a coupon. You'll be amazed by the return.

MR. JAMES: Well...

BOB: Look, give it a whirl. You'll not only be surprised, but you'll be happy too. I won't have to sell you, you'll have to sell me ... ok?

In Bob's case, enthusiasm brought a sale and won over a tough prospect.

How can you increase your earning power by injecting enthusiasm into your sales presentation?

First, force yourself to think enthusiastic thoughts. When you do you'll act enthusiastic.

Second, use your big-thinking formula to double or triple the amount of enthusiasm you have been putting into your work. This, in turn, will double or triple your happiness.

Third, think about how much your product or service will help your prospect. By thinking positive thoughts you'll energize your entire sales talk.

11. ALLOWING PROSPECT TO SLIP AWAY

It's discouraging to activate your big-thinking selling machine, give a dynamite sales presentation, and have a prospect say, "Gee, I'm just not in the market for your product at this time." A turndown, no matter how subtle, shakes your confidence and causes you to question your selling ability.

Every salesperson goes through the trauma of self-doubt, wondering if the selling machine is slowing down. This phase, in most cases, is short lived because salespeople realize they won't sell every prospect.

The real "confidence shaker" comes when a salesperson notices that more and more prospects are saying "no!"

Then it happens. The cerebral interrogation begins with questions like:

Why are my prospects refusing to buy?
Am I "turning off" my prospects?
Are my prospects unimpressed with my sales presentation?

Admittedly, if a prospect doesn't need a product or service or can't afford to make the purchase, he isn't going to be in the market to buy. As these products establish themselves in their business, they tend to want and buy more. So, in time, you can expect to increase your sales earnings *if* you avoid letting your prospects slip away. The following guidelines will help you keep them around:

1. Watch your prospect for early signs of confusion and frustration. A slight wince or head shake should be your signal to run a perception check.

2. Reiterate the strong points of your sales presentation. Make sure your prospect has a clear understanding. If you're not sure, ask questions.

3. Take your time. Don't rush your sales presentation. A relaxed prospect thinks better with a clear head.

4. Convince your prospect that you have his interest at heart. An enthusiastic selling approach will show your prospect that you really care about his welfare.

5. Some prospects take delight in playing hard to sell. They'll give you a rough time to see how long you can last. Hang in there and do the best selling job you can. The prospect, more often than not, will respect your effort and buy your product or service.

6. When a prospect says, "come back later," do just that, but make sure you set a definite time for your return visit. Let your prospect know that you're a serious, big-thinking salesperson.

12. FAILING TO HELP PROSPECT SOLVE PROBLEM

You can't solve a problem unless you're aware one exists. Yet some salespeople insist on bypassing casual conversation and bolting straight ahead into their sales presentation. In doing so, they often don't give a prospect a chance to express an immediate concern. If a prospect reveals a concern early enough, the salesperson can adjust his sales presentation to address the problem.

Can helping a prospect solve a problem work in your favor? Yes, it can. A friend of mine, David Strickland, was a vacuum cleaner representative. He specialized in showing his prospects how to move merchandise. In one case, for instance, he outlined a program for a dealer who had trouble selling merchandise. The dealer sold seventy-eight units in a four-day period. David not only showed the dealer how to do it, but volunteered to work on the floor for two days. As a result, the dealer bought fifty additional units, sold them out, and ordered thirty-five more. By helping the dealer solve a problem, David gained a steady customer—and friend.

In another instance, Martin Youngstedt sold newspaper advertising before switching to selling commercial real estate. His advertisers complained loudly when business slowed down. He would boost their spirits by running an occasional article featuring one of his merchants—pictures, short biography, plans of merchant, and so on. The merchants loved these articles because their customers would pass along favorable comments, thus convincing the merchants that people really do read the newspaper. Therefore, Martin had little trouble keeping a stable of faithful advertisers.

So in order to lend support when needed, keep these guidelines in mind:

1. Help prospect bring problem into the open.
2. Work with prospect in determining cause and effect of problem.
3. Establish a workable plan for solving problem. Take action, but proceed one step at a time.
4. Never give up. If your plan for remediation doesn't succeed, try another.

13. OVERLOADING YOUR SALES PRESENTATION

Some time in your selling career you may have to ask yourself: Should I include more information in my sales presentation or omit certain parts? This question usually surfaces when sales begin to slack off. It will be, for the most part, a tough question to answer.

It's quite possible that you've packed too much extraneous material in your sales presentation, thus causing it to bog down and lose momentum. Here are some trouble spots that may occur:

1. Too many features or highlights presented at one time. A packed sales presentation tends to tire the prospect.
2. Wild, extravagant claims that promise the moon. Unfortunately, many of these statements are nurtured through emotional stimuli.
3. Using a plethora of miracle expressions such as "vastly superior to its nearest competitor" or "heads above anything in its class" or "the greatest thing ever" or "pinnacle of superlative." A product or service, no matter how efficient, runs into problems on occasion. Most prospects are smart enough to realize this and resent being hoodwinked into thinking something is perfect.
4. Packing sales presentation with irrelevant material or items that fail to interest prospect.

The following suggestions will help you keep your sales presentation in top form:

1. Demonstrate one feature of your product or service at a time. Let your prospect absorb and digest the main points.

2. Speak slowly and clearly. Be ready to answer questions with confidence.

3. Avoid padding your sales presentation with extraneous material. Most long-winded presentations do little to excite a prospect. Keep your sales presentation brief, concise, and convincing.

4. Above all, be honest. Prepare yourself to back up any claims you make regarding your product or service. If you don't know the answer to a question, admit it. But be sure to tell your prospect that you'll return with an answer to his question. Then come back with an appropriate response.

14. NEGLECTING TO STRESS MAJOR POINTS IN YOUR SELLING PRESENTATION

Often when a salesperson neglects to emphasize an important point in his sales presentation, the prospect, not having any reason to remember, forgets what has been said. Naturally, it follows that repetition of major ideas gives the prospect a clear picture of what you're trying to say.

As an example, try this experiment: Recite ten words to a friend. After reciting the words have your friend write down the words that he remembers. Will he remember all of the words? Probably not. In fact, you might have to repeat the words three or four times before your friend remembers all of them.

Repetition, then, will help a prospect grasp the ideas and store them in his memory bank. It will also help you sell your product or service. Last point: Use variety with repetition—that is, look for different ways of saying the same thing. Flexibility in your sales approach keeps your prospect alert.

15. NEGLECTING TO ALLOW PROSPECT TO SELL HIMSELF

A big thinker makes the prospect feel as though he's selling himself. The magic comes from creating a pressure-free selling situation.

High-pressure selling methods work like quicksand. They surround and smother a prospect. A trapped prospect does not have the freedom to think clearly or make a firm decision.

When pressure builds, three events often occur: one, the prospect refuses to buy; two, the prospect buys; and three, the prospect buys to get rid of the salesperson, then cancels the order the following day.

There will always be some pressure in selling, but what often hurts a sale is "RA," or resistance arousal. Simply, a prospect reaches a point in the sales presentation where pressure forces him to build barriers and to resist further selling strategies.

Nearly all prospects like to feel free to move and think at their own pace. As a big-thinking salesperson you set the stage for selling success by giving your prospect room to express himself.

An excellent method for getting a prospect to sell himself is to draw out his thoughts and feelings regarding your product or service early in the conversation. By doing so, you can use this same information to get your prospect to agree with your during your sales presentation. How does this work? Let's assume that you're soliciting the services of a CPA. You're talking with Ms. Stewart, prospect.

YOU: Ms. Stewart, do you feel that good bookkeeping is important in a business?

Ms. S: Of course I do.

YOU: Do you feel that it's wise to have a CPA check your records periodically?

Ms.S: No question about it.

YOU: Do feel that financial statements are important to have?

Ms. S: Not really.

YOU: One of my clients tells me that a monthly statement is the most important tool in his business.

Ms. S: Why is that?

YOU: Well, he knows exactly where he stands financially at the end of every month. Also, do you know the first thing his bank asks to see when he applies for a loan?

Ms. S: Oh, yes. A financial statement.

YOU: Sure. And the way business is today, you never know when you'll need a loan.

Let's review the conversation. First of all, Ms. Stewart believes in keeping records and having them checked by a CPA. Second, she agrees, after slight hesitation, that a financial statement can be a definite asset in a business.

If, during the sales presentation, Ms. Stewart stalls or hedges, you can interject with, "Well, Ms. Stewart, as you agreed, it's wise for a CPA to check your records periodically."

You can also ask a direct question and hope your prospect gives the proper response. For example:

YOU: You know, Mr. Palmer, most businessmen like yourself really appreciate the profit and loss statement. My client's services can provide a monthly update on the financial standing of your business. Do you feel this service would be beneficial to you, and if so, how?

MR. P: By all means. I could really use this service. I'd be able to tell at any given time exactly where my business stood financially.

Now if during the sales presenation your prospect offers resistance, you can come back with: "It's like you said, Mr. Palmer, it's nice to know at any given time exactly where you stand." Few prospects continue to resist when they realize such action leads to contradiction.

POINTS TO REMEMBER

Recognizing problems is the first step toward improvement. Establishing a workable plan to solve these problems is the second and most important step in reaching your major selling objective.

A good way to correct these problems is to concentrate on them one at a time. In this way you'll stay alert and continue to seek positive solutions.

Accepting a problem as a personal challenge tests your big-thinking selling ability to overcome obstacles, leave your comfort zone, and meet your career goals.

CHAPTER NINE

BIG-THINKING SELLING STRATEGIES FOR KEEPING YOURSELF ON TARGET

Staying on target requires you, the big-thinking salesperson, to approach each prospect intelligently, to communicate effectively with each prospect, and to conscientiously apply a selling strategy that benefits both you and the prospect.

The chapter will include the following topics:

1. Motivating yourself to sell big
2. Increasing your sales earnings through effective communication
3. How to reach your prospect and express your feelings
4. Are you communicating like a big thinker? (self-test)
5. Using big-thinking psychology when selling a prospect
6. Applying a four-step action plan for effective communication
7. How to improve communication and build trust
8. Persuading your prospect to say yes

1. MOTIVATING YOURSELF TO SELL BIG

Without question, you can't inspire others unless you believe in yourself and your ability to earn big money in selling. Therefore, self-motivation or getting yourself on track should be your first consideration as a big-thinking salesperson.

As an example, picture a stone resting on top of a hill. It attracts little attention because it isn't doing anything noticeable. Now if you give the stone a push, it'll roll down the hill and gradually pick up speed until some outside force causes it to stop.

Unlike a stone, you can't depend on forces, especially those generated by others, to start your selling machine in motion. As a big-thinker, you must explode out of the starting blocks each day, and you must provide your own fuel or energy to keep your selling spirit high. The question is how.

First, review your selling goals each day before you contact your first prospect. This serves as a reminder to think positive, sell with enthusiasm, and assist those in need of your services.

Walter Brady, a salesman, told me that he concentrates on short-term selling goals to keep his motivation high. He said, "I've got to think about those things that I can control at the moment." For instance, he practices the following goal-related strategies:

- Treat my prospect as the most important person in the world
- Sell with the best of my ability
- Sell with confidence, sincerity, and enthusiasm
- Believe wholeheartedly in my product; it's the best on the market today

Walter Brady earns approximately $56,000 a year. One of his long-term, big-thinking goals is to earn $100,000 or more a year. He believes the best way to reach long-term goals is to handle your selling commitments one day at a time. "Many salespeople," says Brady, "miss their targets simply because they don't set up daily incentives. They lose interest and leave selling."

Second, indulge in those activities that give you a constant boost, a warm, springy feeling inside. Perhaps a happy thought about an upcoming event or simply saying "good morning" to a friend will energize your selling system and make you feel good for the rest of the day. Often it's the simplest, least expensive experience that pays the highest dividends.

Third, music, for many salespeople, acts as a positive stimulus to get them in a comfortable selling mood. Ben Neuhouse, a salesman, listens to songs from *My Fair Lady* every morning while getting ready for work. He says that music makes him feel warm all over and gives him quick energy. He listens to a mixture of rock and western music between calls. "What you listen to isn't important," states Ben, "as long as it gives you the lift you need."

Psychologically speaking, soft, soothing music provides a carefree, relaxing atmosphere. Both salesperson and prospect can think and speak clearly under these conditions. Ben told me that his sales earnings increased by forty percent since he learned to relax and shake off the pressure of meeting a prospect for the first time.

Fourth, read your daily affirmations (Chapter 4) and repeat them over to yourself. See yourself as a big-thinking success, and at the same time make new friends.

Fifth, when exciting things happen to you, share these experiences with others. Their moral support will give you the impetus to do more. *Note:* You won't always receive a standing ovation from others. Some people allow jealousy to stifle their responses. Undoubtedly, the best person to rely on is yourself.

2. INCREASING YOUR SALES EARNINGS THROUGH EFFECTIVE COMMUNICATION

Talking with others. Expressing yourself in simple terms. Listening intently to what others are saying. Together these actions form the backbone of effective communication. And next to self-motivation, effective communication spells the difference between earning big money in selling and limping about from month to month wondering why sales aren't improving.

The next six sections will help you to strengthen your communicating skills.

3. HOW TO REACH YOUR PROSPECT AND EXPRESS YOUR FEELINGS

A big thinker views each prospect through a positive eye. Yet not all prospects need or want or intend to purchase the product or service. Your success often hinges on how you contact your prospect and relay your feelings.

Study the following situations and think how you would react:

a. Your prospect responds in a cold, standoffish manner. You feel tense and unsure of yourself. What would you say? How would you express yourself without words?

b. Constant interruptions break the flow of your sales presentation. Nothing seems to be going right. What would you say? How would you express yourself without words?

c. Your prospect acts confused. He doesn't know whether or not to purchase your product. What would you say? How would you express yourself without words?

d. Your prospect demands flawless service, a perfect product, and a thirty-percent discount. What would you say? How would you express yourself without words?

In most cases your reaction to these situations would depend on your present attitude, your desire to make a sale, and your ability to adapt quickly to changing events.

It's tough to stay calm and think positive when a prospect gives you a hard time. However, as a big-thinking salesperson, you must keep a clear head and respond in an enthusiastic fashion. Your verbal and nonverbal expressions reveal how you honestly feel about your prospect and the selling scene.

You can verbally demonstrate your feelings to a prospect in the following ways:

- State your position. Let your prospect know how you feel about your product or service and what you intend to accomplish during the meeting.

- Be assertive. Say what is on your mind without putting your prospect in an embarrassing or defensive position.

- Speak in a polite, cordial manner. Show understanding and compassion by allowing your prospect to converse freely.

Experiments suggest that many people will judge you before they get to know you or learn how you feel about certain issues. They form their opinions solely by your nonverbal actions; that is, how you stand, your facial expressions, how you walk or sit, and so on.

Here are four nonverbal expressions that work well in selling:

1. Give your prospect some breathing room. Stand far enough away to allow him plenty of personal space. This shows consideration and respect for your prospect.

2. Show confidence by standing tall and erect.

3. Smile. A smiling, happy face invites your prospect to relax.

4. Look your prospect in the eye when talking or listening to him. Eye contact is a vital cue for letting your know how your prospect feels about your sales presentation. For example, if your prospect looks away, he may be bored or he may want to express an idea or opinion. People of course react in different ways. If your prospect seems confused or uncomfortable, stop your presentation and find out what the problem is. In this way, both you and your prospect help each other to stay together during the presentation.

One of the best ways to reach your prospect is to say what you want and the reason why. After your sales presentation, for instance, you might say something like this:

> "Ms. Russell, take the product. And please do it now. Our prices are going up next month," or "You know, Mr. Danelli, our service fits your needs perfectly. I'd like to sign you up now. The sooner we start, the more we'll accomplish."

This approach "forces" an immediate response from the prospect, bypassing call backs and unnecessary delays. Don't confuse this strategy with high-pressure tactics. Remember, you're working with a qualified prospect who has a definite need that your product or service can meet. Also, your prospect can afford to purchase your product or service.

4. ARE YOU COMMUNICATING LIKE A BIG THINKER? (A SELF-TEST)

That's a good question. And you can find the answer if you take a pencil and a sheet of paper and select the choice that you would be more likely to use for each of the following items:

1. A. There are times when I hurry through my sales presentation.
   B. I try to make every minute count. I pace myself and make sure my prospect understands what I am saying and doing.

2. A. I stick to a certain plan of action. Switching strategies in the middle of a sales presentation weakens the sales approach.

   B. I stay flexible by mentally preparing myself to use an alternative plan if necessary.

3. A. I try to provide a relaxed selling atmosphere.

   B. I like a prospect to get "fired up" and argue. It makes the selling scene more challenging and exciting.

4. A. I try to agree with the prospect at all times.

   B. If I feel my prospect is wrong, I attempt to explain why.

5. A. I assert my wishes, but try to find an intermediate position between my prospect's and mine.

   B. Even if my prospect is wrong, I don't believe in creating tension by proving my point.

6. A. I show the strengths of my product or service, never the shortcomings.

   B. I make sure my prospect knows the pros and cons of my product or service.

7. A. I try to understand my prospect's point of view and show empathy for his position.

   B. I believe most prospects aren't sure what they want and need to be shown.

8. A. Since my prospect has a mind of his own, I try not to influence the way he thinks.

   B. I attempt to get my prospect to agree with me.

9. A. Often I exaggerate and make wild claims about my product or service. After all, prospects expect it from salespeople.

   B. I feel that even a slight exaggeration or two may ruin my credibility with my prospect.

10. A. I concentrate on one issue at a time during my sales presentation. In this way I avoid confusing my prospect.

   B. Shifting from one item to another is a good sales presentation technique. It gives a prospect a full understanding of my product or service.

A big thinker's answers: 1. B; 2. B; 3. A; 4. B; 5. A; 6. B; 7. A; 8. B; 9. B; 10. A.

This self-test points up the key factors a big thinker employs for effective communication. They are: 1) adjusting the sales presentation to fit the needs and interests of the prospect; 2) proper pacing, making each moment count; 3) planning in advance what to say and how to say it; 4) making mental preparations to switch directions, if applicable; 5) providing a comfortable selling atmosphere; 6) empathizing and attempting to understand the prospect's point of view; 7) providing a full understanding (strengths and weaknesses) of the product or service; and 8) concentrating on one sales feature at a time.

5. USING BIG-THINKING PSYCHOLOGY WHEN SELLING A PROSPECT

A big thinker sets the selling stage for positive action by working with and for the prospect. Leonard L. Murdy wrote, "We have grown to where we are through our relationships with people. We will grow to what we will be through our relationships with people." In short, you'll reach your major selling objective if you cater directly to your prospect's needs.

We've mentioned that part of big-thinking strategy is to hit your prospect with one issue at a time. It shows your prospect that you know your product or service and wish to pass along valuable information in a thorough, well-thought-out fashion. Sidetracking or digressing in several directions tends to confuse your prospect and demonstrates a lack of organization on your part.

A big thinker also stays away from the "overpositive sales trap." This occurs when a salesperson sees his product or service as being perfect, the pinnacle of superlative. This narrow-minded view can cause problems. If a prospect, for example, refutes or challenges something the salesperson says, the salesperson may make the mistake of arguing with the prospect, thus allowing emotion to enter the selling scene. A big thinker handles this situation by listening to the prospect, analyzing the motivation behind the prospect's concern, and reinforcing his position without losing control.

In reality, big-thinking psychology is little more than common sense, intelligence, and an awareness of what is going on around you. Being yourself and allowing others to express themselves in a pressure-free atmosphere promotes big sales, over and over again.

6. APPLYING A FOUR-STEP ACTION PLAN FOR EFFECTIVE COMMUNICATION

Effective communication means that you and your prospect understand and respect each other's ideas, opinions, and feelings. Communication requires a concentrated effort on the part of both parties.

Let's examine a four-step action plan that you can readily apply to improve your communicating skills.

1. Paraphrasing—Listen carefully to what your prospect is saying; then repeat the major points in your own words. Ask your prospect, "Am I understanding you correctly?" This approach assures your prospect that you are truly interested in him.

2. Describing behavior—Report specific, observable actions of your prospect without interpretation or value judgments. As an example, you say to your prospect, "You know, Ms. Tracey, your eyes grew like saucers when you heard that last statement," or "Ms. Knowles, you stiffened your entire body when your husband agreed to take our service." This approach allows your prospect to respond without feeling intimidated or forced to defend any specific action.

3. Perception checking—Study the verbal and nonverbal actions of your prospect. When you are not sure how your prospect feels about something, ask. For example, you might inquire, "You're not completely satisfied with what I just said, are you?" By doing this you transform your prospect's expression of feeling into a tentative description of feeling.

4. Giving and receiving feedback—Feedback occurs when you report your observations and reactions to your prospect. Let's say, for instance, that Mr. Stanlerd, your prospect, hasn't received his order from your company. Here's what you might say to your prospect: "Your order, Mr. Stanlerd, is being processed again. You wouldn't believe what happened the first time. But don't worry. I'll see to it that you receive your order on time. Is that okay with you?"

Your prospect, as a receiver of feedback, might respond to your statement by asking a question or suggesting that you give him additional information. For example:

MR. STANLERD: Oh, really, what did happen to my order? Now you've pushed my curiosity button.

Obviously, feedback is essentially an ongoing conversational process between two or more people. The quality of feedback depends on the awareness and concern of those involved.

As a salesperson, you use these techniques to communicate on a daily basis. Yet, it's easy for you, as it is for many salespeople, to become lazy, go through the motions, and think there isn't any reason to evaluate the effectiveness of your communicating skills.

You can avoid this problem by constantly studying your Self-Analysis Checklist (Chapter 2), monitoring the progress of your sales production, and structuring an exercise to help you improve your skills.

Your exercise may simply be to concentrate on what your prospect says by mentally repeating the words over in your mind. Then run a perception check by repeating in your own words what you heard your prospect say. Study your prospect's reaction, describe the behavior, and tactfully employ feedback to keep the flow of conversation moving at a brisk pace.

7. HOW TO IMPROVE COMMUNICATION AND BUILD TRUST

You can improve your communication skills and build trust by committing yourself to action. The steps are as follows:

- Make a list of the communication skills that you need to work on.
- Prioritize the list; that is, place the most important item at the top of the list, and so forth.
- Write down how you intend to seek improvement.
- Record the targeted completion date for each skill.
- Record evidence of success.

Copy the action plan format in Figure 9-1 on a piece of paper. You'll need a pen or pencil and ruler. Then fill in the appropriate spaces.

Figure 9-1

COMMUNICATION PLAN OF ACTION

What I need to work on	What I will do to improve	Target completion date	Evidence of success
1. Perception checking—become more aware of prospect's feelings, etc.	1. Listen carefully, paraphrase my prospect's words.	1. Open; this is a daily, ongoing process.	1. Building a stronger rapport with prospects. Sales beginning to improve.
2.	2.	2.	2.
3.	3.	3.	3.

One reason big-thinking salespeople double or triple their earnings is that they commit themselves to big-thinking action. They don't bask in pipe dreams or sit around and visualize themselves as leaders in the selling profession. They constantly search out and destroy those "negatrons" that are famous for inhibiting your selling progress.

8. PERSUADING YOUR PROSPECT TO SAY YES

Let's review a common-sense selling strategy for getting your prospect to buy. Here's an eight-point plan that brings successful results:

1. Create a positive selling atmosphere—walk in with a smile; show enthusiasm.
2. Use a gentle, confident tone of voice; choose your words wisely.
3. Show empathy and compassion for your prospect's situation.
4. Listen to and understand your prospect's point of view. Put yourself in his position.
5. Agree with your prospect. Get him on your side. Then work with him to identify specific needs.
6. Now get your prospect to agree with you; that is, after establishing a need, set up a workable plan to help him find a positive solution.
7. Urge your prospect to act now by making a commitment to buy your product or service.
8. Ask for the sale. Have a definite closing strategy in mind.

POINTS TO REMEMBER

See yourself as a big-thinking success. Then work hard to achieve that goal by motivating yourself to be the best salesperson you can possibly be.

How can you motivate yourself? By doing five basic things. They are: One, review your selling goals on a daily basis; two, keep yourself on a mental "high"; three, activate a pleasing stimulus such as music to put you in a happy mood; four, study your daily affirmations; and five, share favorable experiences with others.

Examine your own style of communicating and structure a plan to help you improve your skills. Strengthen your ability to accurately describe behavior, paraphrase the words of others, run perception checks, and give and receive feedback.

Finally, commit yourself to practice positive communication, follow up by checking your progress, and let nothing interfere with your personal growth.

CHAPTER TEN

RECOGNIZING AND PREVENTING SELLING BURNOUT

I n recent years the term *burnout* has creeped into the literature. Newspapers and magazines carry articles about job burnout— its causes, symptoms, and cures. In fact, books offering preventive measures and sure-fire remedies for keeping job burnout at a safe distance are appearing on the shelves.

In this chapter we'll investigate job burnout and what effect it has on people in the selling profession. We'll examine the following areas:

1. What is selling burnout?
2. Are you a potential burnout victim? (a test)
3. What are the symptoms of selling burnout?
4. How does selling burnout take control?
5. What part does stress play in selling burnout?
6. Treating the symptoms of selling burnout
7. Finding the underlying causes of burnout
8. A big thinker's techniques for preventing selling burnout

Let's begin by examining the term *burnout*.

1. WHAT IS SELLING BURNOUT?

Selling burnout is a condition in which a salesperson no longer finds selling challenging, interesting, or profitable. Just the thought of getting up in the morning and going to work depresses the salesperson. Burnout seldom occurs all at once. It, like slow-rising flood water, takes time to settle in and spread out. Basically, the salesperson is unhappy with his work, his associates, his boss, and perhaps most of all, himself. He often becomes lethargic and does barely enough to get by. He survives from day to day and has little or no ambition.

In education, teachers call burnout the "big click," which means that the guiding light has gone out and darkness prevails. Athletic coaches refer to burnout as the "final gun" or the "last lap around the track." Unequivocally speaking, no matter what it's called, burnout does more to discourage big thinking than anything else.

2. ARE YOU A POTENTIAL BURNOUT VICTIM? (A TEST)

Even as a big-thinking salesperson you must keep a watchful eye on anything that might open the door to burnout. Notice the word "potential" in the headline. For our purposes "potential" means "in the process of developing."

You are going to take a true/false quiz. Number 1 through 20 on a sheet of paper. Read each question carefully, and place a *T* for *True* or *F* for *False* on your answer sheet after the number. Answer questions as honestly as you can.

1. Do you *frequently* wish that you had a different job, perhaps in another location?
2. Are you growing tired of doing the "same old thing"?
3. Is your present job creating problems at home for you?
4. Do you *often* feel that your efforts go unnoticed or that you are not appreciated?
5. Are you experiencing more on-the-job conflicts than ever before?
6. Do you sincerely believe that your fellow workers are given better treatment than you?
7. Is your enthusiasm slipping; that is, do you have a hard time getting your selling machine started?
8. Are you having trouble reaching your personal selling goals?
9. Do you purposely avoid hard-to-sell prospects?

10. Do you find yourself bringing work problems home with you?

11. Do you seem to be working harder and receiving fewer benefits?

12. Do you find yourself making important decisions in a matter-of-fact fashion?

13. Are you becoming more argumentative or short-tempered lately?

14. Do you find yourself working just hard enough to get by?

15. Are you getting increased pressure at home to advance more quickly on your job?

16. Is there steady pressure on you to make more sales?

17. Does your present job lack variety or flexibility?

18. Are you finding it increasingly more difficult to climb out of bed and go to work?

19. Are you living up to your own expectations?

20. Do you *often* question your ability to succeed as a big-thinking salesperson?

A *yes* answer to any of these questions *may* indicate the onset of selling burnout. Perhaps a better understanding of the problem will come in the next section as we discuss the symptoms of selling burnout.

3. WHAT ARE THE SYMPTOMS OF SELLING BURNOUT?

Some burnout symptoms are easier to recognize than others since they signal a turnabout or switch from the normal selling routine. These obvious changes tip-off the selling machine that it's time for a tuneup, or even a complete overhaul.

Here are eight noticeable symptoms for selling burnout:

1. The selling process becomes monotonous—too much of the same old thing.

2. Selling no longer provides a challenge. One sale is just like another. There isn't any novelty or thrill in filling out a customer order.

3. Fellow workers aren't fun to be around any more; their presence often creates tension and anxiety.

4. There is mounting pressure from others to increase sales production.

5. Enthusiasm dwindles. That burning desire to sell, sell, sell slowly fades into oblivion.

6. It becomes easier (mentally and physically) to expend a minimum effort and settle for mediocrity.

7. Problems and conflicts are passed along to others. Unwillingness to accept any responsibility for finding workable solutions. Apathetic toward suggestions.

8. A negative attitude controls the thought process. The salesperson expects little, gains little, and badmouths others when things go awry.

Let's go one step further by listing major burnout symptoms along with the agents that are partly responsible for creating these symptoms.

BURNOUT SYMPTOMS	USUALLY CREATED BECAUSE SALESPERSON...
Boredom sets in; selling becomes drudgery.	feels efforts go unrecognized; others gain advantage.
Fading competitive spirit.	content with minimum recognition.
Associates try patience; bring on feelings of cynicism and skepticism.	either dislikes fellow workers or feels supervisor favors associates.
Pressure from others to do better.	isn't putting forth a satisfactory effort, thus sales dip and earnings drop off.
Enthusiasm gives way to apathy.	either sets unrealistic goals or no selling goals at all.
Does only enough to survive.	feels he's going nowhere in his selling career.

BURNOUT SYMPTOMS	USUALLY CREATED BECAUSE SALESPERSON...
Loss of ambition and initiative.	isn't serious about becoming a big-thinking salesperson.
Expectancy dial turned on low; negative thoughts prevail.	wants out of selling.
Increased absenteeism.	has little or no desire to go to work.
Unwilling to cooperate or work on innovative projects.	only concerned with putting in time and going home.
Constant complaining about work conditions, treatment by supervisors, and so on.	feels others are "out to get him."
Feel efforts go unnoticed. Nobody appreciates hard work.	receives virtually no accolades for expended energy.

Now let's see how selling burnout, like erosion, gradually wears down a salesperson.

4. HOW DOES SELLING BURNOUT TAKE CONTROL?

Selling burnout symptoms gain a solid foothold when a salesperson loses motivation to sell, develops a poor self-image, or fails to reach major personal goals within a reasonable length of time.

Why do these events occur? Let's look at each one. First, psychologists refer to motivation as an inner state of arousal toward a goal. So it follows that if a salesperson's pilot light flickers or dies out, the drive to continue wilts like a day-old lettuce salad.

What factors cause this inner state of arousal to fade? Here are three common ones:

1. The salesperson reports a lack of positive strokes from significant others—that is, manager, spouse, peers, par-

ents, and so on. His accomplishments become matter-of-fact, and at best may only muster an occasional "Gee, that's nice."

2. The salesperson may begin to feel that what he's doing really isn't that important. After all, it's only a living, nothing outstanding or exciting.

3. The salesperson takes on a feeling of helplessness. He may believe that others—prospects, family members, company officials—are not benefiting from his efforts.

These situations may invite stagnation to replace motivation. And once this happens, frustration eventually takes over.

Second, a salesperson may develop a poor self-image, especially if sales drop or show no significant improvement over a period of time. The salesperson, feeling that he's standing still, seriously questions his future as a big-thinking salesperson. His coworkers may kiddingly refer to him as "Ace" or "Flash." These remarks cut deeply and further convince the salesperson that he's fading fast.

Third, the salesperson fails to reach personal selling goals. At first he might have little trouble meeting or surpassing daily, weekly, or monthly goals. Then, as time passes, he sees himself falling behind and relying on defense mechanisms to excuse his lack of progress.

Now let's suppose that you detect these burnout symptoms in your selling program. What can you do about it? Here are six suggestions that big-thinking salespeople find effective:

1. Rely on others for moral support, but don't expect congratulations for everything you do. Establish a workable selling program around realistic personal goals. As you reach these goals, pat yourself on the back; others either forget or are too involved with their own projects to pass along timely accolades.

2. Change activities often. Include enough fresh ideas so you have something to look forward to each day.

3. Take an active part in planning your selling program. Stay in control and direct your energies toward your stated goals.

4. Build on your successes. Use them as steps in your upward climb.

5. Seek challenging events. Keep your mind and body busy. This prevents you from becoming locked into doing the same old thing.

6. Capitalize on your strengths. Continue to improve upon the things you do well.

5. WHAT PART DOES STRESS PLAY IN SELLING BURNOUT?

Stress plays a vital role in a salesperson's life because it often determines what direction he will take. Unfortunately, as stress builds the salesperson may feel his job lacks the challenge he needs to feed his competitive urge. He may feel that his skills are being wasted.

Stress hits people in different ways. A salesperson may think that he's worth far more than others choose to believe. This disparity tends to create hard feelings and puts everyone on edge.

Stressors, those events responsible for building tension, are not always noticeable or easy to handle once they are recognized as problem areas. Yet when they occur and establish themselves as stressors, the cycle illustrated in Figure 10-1 appears:

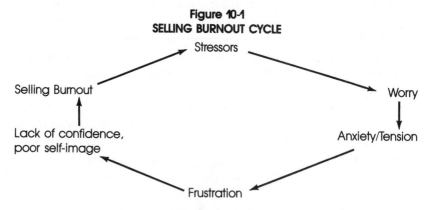

Figure 10-1
SELLING BURNOUT CYCLE

Here are eight situations that invite stressors to enter and take hold:

1. The salesperson works at almost a fanatical pace. He tries

to do too much. The energy valve remains wide open and the selling machine pumps overtime.

2. The salesperson relies on others to provide mental support and expects them to come through during rough times. He does not prepare himself for an alternate course in case his friends let him down.

3. The salesperson worries too much about the problems of others. His troubleshooting efforts sap his mental and physical energy.

4. The salesperson shuts out others and becomes easily disturbed when those around him interrupt his work. He wants to be left alone to progress at his own pace.

5. The salesperson's yearly earnings fall short of his expectations. His dreams crumble like a dry cookie, causing him to consider alternative ways of earning a living.

6. The salesperson works in a crowded office. He feels hurried, always rushing about to stay on schedule. Frequently it takes him an hour or so to unwind once he arrives home.

7. The salesperson's health has been declining in recent months. It becomes increasingly more difficult to put in a full day's work. Pressure builds as family members and coworkers express their concern regarding the salesperson's future.

8. The salesperson feels stagnation taking over, since his job offers little or no variety. Doing the same thing day after day is slowing snuffing out his desire to excel.

6. TREATING THE SYMPTOMS OF SELLING BURNOUT

Once the salesperson recognizes possible burnout symptoms and girds himself to eliminate them, he's well on his way to big-thinking success.

What can you do to treat selling burnout symptoms should they develop? Experts say the following treatments bring pleasing results for most people:

1. Organize your mind for success. Expect temporary set-backs; in fact, use them as learning experiences to strengthen your selling machine. Conditioning your mind for success requires you to drop old, ineffective selling habits for new, effective ones. This is a tough order because an old habit hangs on like a stubborn cold. Often an old habit is hard to break. You've grown accustomed to behaving in a certain manner and feel comfortable doing so. It's almost like a golfer with a terrible swing who resists learning a new swing because it would mean slow progress and high golf scores. In time the improved swing would reduce his score, but his present swing gets him through a game with a passable score.

2. Plan nice things for yourself and others. For example, write a friend a note or letter praising his or her strengths. You'll feel good and your friend will respond in kind. Talk to others about your plans for the future. Share innovative ideas with them. Keep a steady line of communication going with those who influence your way of thinking. This gives you something useful and interesting to look forward to each day.

3. Leave your work at the office, especially on days when nothing seems to go right. Spend quality time at home with loved ones.

4. Develop an interesting hobby, one that can be shared with others from time to time. A hobby helps fill leisure time with happy thoughts and takes your mind off of stressful events.

5. Just relax. Read, listen to music, watch a sporting event, go to a movie, or do anything that brings enjoyment and peace of mind.

6. Set up rewards for yourself as your reach certain goals—go out to dinner or plan an exciting weekend, for example. Include a special person to enjoy these moments with. This will give you the incentive to improve your big-thinking selling skills.

7. If all fails, think seriously about changing jobs. Maybe selling isn't right for you after all.

7. FINDING THE UNDERLYING CAUSES OF BURNOUT

As a salesperson you may be fully aware that burnout symptoms are gnawing away at your selling machine, but the problem is why? After all, you've been selling for years, and with a few exceptions, have felt moderately secure.

You can apply the big thinker's breakdown plan to pinpoint trouble spots. You need three sheets of paper, a pencil or pen, and a ruler. Now do the following:

One, draw two columns on a sheet of paper. Label the first column *Things I don't like about my job*, and the second column *Things I do like about my job*. A sample is provided in Figure 10-2.

Figure 10-2

Things I don't like about my job.	Things I do like about my job.
1. My supervisor is always in a hurry; I feel uncomfortable in her presence.	1. Incentive bonuses; excellent reward system.
2. Crowded office space.	2. Company has a good reputation.
3. Management doesn't acknowledge Suggestion Box.	3. Small staff turnover.

Fill in the spaces with appropriate answers.

Two, draw two columns on a second sheet of paper. Label the first column *What I can do to make things better* and the second column *What I can't do to make things better*. A sample is provided in Figure 10-3.

Figure 10-3

What I can do to make things better.	What I can't do to make things better.
1. Speak directly to the supervisor. Let him or her know that improvement is needed in certain areas.	1. Demand or push for immediate changes without going through proper channels or approaching the problem in a sensible manner.
2. Offer your assistance in any way possible.	

Fill in the spaces with appropriate answers.

Three, write the following statement on a third sheet of paper: *How I plan to change the things I don't like and can do something about.* Sample answers are provided in Figure 10-4.

Figure 10-4

How I plan to change the things I don't like and can do something about.
1. Try to understand my supervisor by getting to know her better. Attend social functions and carry on casual conversation with supervisor. Find out special interests, hobbies, etc., of supervisor.
2. Ask that Suggestion Box responses be read and acted upon at regular staff meetings.

By following a written plan that requires sound thinking and careful analysis, you can uncover the hidden factors that are responsible for causing burnout symptoms.

8. A BIG-THINKER'S TECHNIQUES FOR PREVENTING SELLING BURNOUT

The ideal situation, of course, would be to love selling so much that you can hardly wait to jump out of bed and go to work. Yes, there are people who devote their lives on a twenty-four hour basis to their jobs. These people have three things in common: They consistently put forth a strong effort, they seek continual improvement, and being a success is their number-one priority. These values, set into goal statements and backed with a burning desire to reach the top, are the key factors that big-thinking salespeople use to reach their major selling objectives.

In review, let's examine how big-thinking magic can prevent selling burnout from taking over.

1. Keep moving ahead. Take each hurdle one jump at a time.

2. Continually seek better ways to sell your product or service. This will keep you occupied and interested in your work.

3. When pressure builds, take frequent rest breaks. Let your mind and body work in unison, free from anxiety and tension.

4. Give yourself continual mental baths. Read updated magazines and books that offer a fresh approach to selling. Read autobiographies of highly successful people. Not only can you benefit from the experiences of others, but their stories serve to inspire confidence. You receive firsthand information on how these people overcame adversity, the negative stimuli that reinforces burnout symptoms, and reached the top of their profession.

5. Recognize and treat your selling territory as an opportunity to expand your selling career. Study your present territory and create new ways to approach old customers with modern ideas. Devise a fresh sales presentation and breathe life into your product or service. Go back to those prospects who failed to buy your product or service; get to know them, find out what they need, and offer assistance. This strategy will reduce or completely wipe out the monotony of everyday selling.

6. Offer your services to other salespeople. Share tips and suggestions for improving selling techniques. Open-minded people learn and profit from each other's experiences.

7. Set your personal selling goals within the scope of reality. Adjust them to correspond with your ability, experience, and ambition. Make them challenging, but not impossible to reach.

8. Monitor your progress on a regular basis. Refer to your *Master Selling Plan*. Make sure that you are taking big-thinking measures to stay on track. Study your *Self-Analysis Checklist*. If you spot problems, take care of them immediately. Remember, big-thinking results require big-thinking action.

9. Keep a sense of humor. Don't take yourself or your product or service too seriously. Levity helps take the tension out of tight situations.

10. Be willing to learn. Dedicate yourself to becoming the best salesperson you can possibly be. Work hard, practice hard, and sell hard.

11. Above all, stay positive in everything you do.

POINTS TO REMEMBER

Burnout is for real. Many salespeople choose to ignore the symptoms or simply pass them off as "part of the job."

The key to preventing burnout from entering your selling program is to stay mentally and physically alert, be flexible in your work habits, welcome variety, and be on the constant lookout for fresh, new ideas. Love what you do and try to make things better for everyone.

Finally, rely on the Four *D's*—determination, dedication, desire, and discipline—to carry you to the top.

If you conscientiously apply the tips and suggestions outlined in this book, you'll become a first-rate, big-thinking salesperson.

You just can't miss.